Latinas in
PUBLIC RELATIONS

Shaping Communications, Communities, and Culture

Melissa Vela-Williamson

Latinas in PUBLIC RELATIONS

For more information visit:

Fig Factor Media | www.figfactormedia.com
Latinas in Public Relations | www.latinasinpr.com

Cover Design by DG Marco Álvarez
Layout by LDG Juan Manuel Serna Rosales

Printed in the United States of America

ISBN: 978-1-961600-35-5
Library of Congress Number: 2024926955

FIG
FACTOR
MEDIA

To Latinas working in public relations and the Latinitas who may join us. We applaud you and welcome you to the highest level of the PR club!

Table of Contents

Foreword

Public relations pros are, above all, great storytellers, and Melissa Vela-Williamson knows this better than anyone. Stories connect us, shape us, and illustrate who we become.

My story is simple but significant. It almost sounds like a fairytale! Once upon a time, there was a little girl growing up in Mexico City with a fig tree in her backyard. One day, she noticed a juicy, ripe fig on one of the branches she could reach. To her, the fig was glorious and much too delightful not to share. She picked it off the tree and saw a man walking past her house. Inspiration struck, and that insignificant fig became the first thing the little girl ever sold. It ignited a passion in her for persuading others, looking them in the eye, and telling them, "I have something amazing for you." That initial spark grew into a hot career in sales after I moved to the United States at 14 years old.

I have been telling this story for twenty years now, even as I have grown from a career in sales to a career in marketing. I still delight in sharing something of significant value with others—the story of a brand or a product. When I discovered public relations (PR), it truly resonated with me because PR juxtaposes sales and storytelling. Instead of asking someone to do something, you are telling them a story that inspires a new thought, belief or behavior. You provoke others to take action in a visceral way.

I am a big believer in storytelling, which is why I have empowered hundreds of authors to tell theirs in our many anthologies at Fig Factor Media. Public relations honed my passion for storytelling and allowed me to take a step further into this world by launching our publishing company in 2014. When people hear stories of a hero's triumphant journey, an underdog who wins against the odds, or someone finally reaching a dream after years of hard work, it makes them feel like anything is possible.

PR is now our bread and butter at my marketing firm, JJR Marketing. I enjoy creating an environment where people can see, hear, or touch a message and feel compelled to engage in relationships or take action. When a news outlet features one of my clients, it creates a golden, positive third-party endorsement that carries weight and opens doors. Magic is always around the corner, so my job is to provoke these micromoments of opportunity on behalf of my clients.

As someone working in the same industry as Melissa and the 14 contributing authors you'll meet in these pages, I find *Latinas in Public Relations* fascinating. I have watched Melissa be an advocate for the industry and win accolades. When we met, I felt an amazing connection because I could feel her passion shining through in all she did. We were kindred spirits from the start, and she inspired me with how she elevated others. Together, we wondered, were there more of us? This book answers the question definitively. This is Melissa's second book but this time, it is not just her story, but also the stories of other Latinas across the nation in this influential industry.

I am honored to have the opportunity to bring this book to the masses. In a world where news media increasingly impacts all areas of society, this book shows communicators and activators of stories that positive change can take root when presented with passion and presence. I know you will enjoy these stories of PR professionals and find them as inspiring as I did. Kudos to all the great communicators out there who are elevating others by telling their stories in impactful ways. PR professionals rock the world, especially you, Melissa!

Jacqueline Ruiz
Founder of Fig Factor Media Publishing, JJR Marketing and The Fig Factor Foundation; Author of 36 books, International Speaker, Pilot

Introduction

This book has been coming for a long time. I just didn't realize it! The main points in this introduction have been stirring in me for at least a decade. I have been stacking thoughts, stats, and stories about the state of Latinas for years. But these thoughts weren't organized yet, and I hadn't found the right outlet to publish my ideas. I bet the stories you'll read from the Latina authors featured in this first-ever public relations (PR) anthology may have been in their hearts for just as long!

What message about Latinas have I wanted to share for years? What impactful words would I share with Latinas if given the chance? It's been a challenge to articulate that message concisely. But this book—a collection of wisdom, industry tips, and hard truths—emerged as the right vehicle to drive forward my rallying cry to Latinas.

I started my career like many Latinas who work in public relations—without academic training. My first years in PR were humbling. I quickly learned how much I didn't know, like the basics of writing PR materials, pitching journalists, strategic approaches, and creating a communications plan. More than two decades later, I have worked in agency, nonprofit, and corporate settings and now lead my boutique firm, MVW Communications. After working with over one hundred brands, I feel confident about my PR know-how. At the beginning of my career, I couldn't imagine I'd be advising anyone, but now I'm sought after for advice, training, and thought leadership.

One of the most impactful ways I share my tips for the field is through writing. My first book, *Smart Talk: Public Relations Essentials All Pros Should Know*, is full of all the skills, industry vocabulary, and models I wish I had known about before I started my career. It also encourages people from diverse backgrounds to enter PR and advance their craft and roles. I wrote that book in response to an internal calling during the COVID-19 pandemic to leave behind a guide in case anything happened to me. The response I received from audiences across the country shows there's a need for more advice and points of view in the PR industry.

Another way I connect with practitioners is through my work as a national columnist for the Public Relations Society of America (PRSA). Since 2020, I have written close to forty columns about cultural strategy. I was the first columnist to ever focus on the Hispanic and Latino market. Given the Latino market's large population and economic power, why is that so? Unfortunately, trying to determine why Latinos are missing in so many aspects of US representation has been a recurring question across much of what I have read, thought about, and experienced in the last few decades.

How I came to write that column is a story in itself. I essentially pitched the editor on offering a consistent voice from and about the Hispanic and Latino communities. Perhaps that's a part of why Latinos, particularly Latinas, are missing from visible vantage points. We're waiting to be asked instead of asking for what we want.

A DEMOGRAPHIC SHIFT IS COMING

Public relations plays an important part in the marketplace and society. How pros craft messages, guide organizations, keep information flowing with external audiences, and decide who gets spotlighted can influence the public's perception. True PR practitioners are not spin doctors. They ethically advise what people should do in many significant situations.

Practicing PR by understanding how people think, feel, and behave is important. This means all PR pros must be culturally competent enough to tailor their communication approach to make different individuals and groups feel respected and included.

Even with a stated undercount, the latest US Census showed that people in the United States are more multiracial than ever. For the first time in history, the white population decreased. The population growth of 22.7 million people was led by respondents who identified as Hispanic or Latino. All stats point to a continued growth in the Latino population and for the white population—the former majority—to comprise less than half of the population in just over two decades. The Hispanic or Latino population is currently the largest racial or ethnic minority group in the country. It is on track to become the majority of the US population over time as the white population decreases. The use of "majority" and "minority" in Census copy is already being modified.

According to Pew Research Center, in 2022, Hispanics made up nearly one in five people in the U.S. (19 percent) and are projected to be one in four by 2060. As researchers from

Arizona State University reported, US Hispanic Latino labor is responsible for $3.2 trillion of the nation's gross domestic product, and Latino purchasing power is measured at $3.4 trillion.

WHY THIS MATTERS IN PR

In PR, the most elite practitioners can "see around the corner" and forecast what changes are coming. Numbers prove it is vital we learn more about the Latino community, embrace this understanding in our work, and elevate practitioners who offer a specialty with this growing consumer base.

Given the current and expected population growth, the inclusion of Latinos in PR should at least equal the representation of Latinos in the United States. But that's not the case. In 2022, the Bureau of Labor Statistics (BLS) showed that people of color in the PR industry made up only 26 percent of the entire practicing field. Of that total, about 11 percent of practitioners identified as Hispanic or Latino versus 19 percent of the population. To come up with the percentage of Latinas in PR, let's do some estimating:

- If roughly 11 percent of PR pros identify as Hispanic/Latino, then a portion of those pros are female—Latinas.
- Given that about 64 percent of US PR pros identify as women, then it stands to reason that about 64 percent of that 11 percent Latino group would be Latina.
- That could mean that Latinas in PR make up about 7 percent of the field.

- Then, if you examine how many Latina pros are at the leadership level, BLS trends would suggest that we have to deduct around 50 percent of that 7 percent.
- So roughly 3.5 percent of Latina pros are estimated to be PR managers or above.

Why is Latina representation in PR low, and at the leadership level even lower? In San Antonio, where I reside, it's fairly common to see Latinas working in public relations. San Antonio is said to be the largest Hispanic-majority city in the United States. At the PRSA San Antonio meetings, you'll see a wide range of Hispanic and Latino practitioners. But that representation drops at the leadership level, and whenever I have tried to find a bilingual Latina PR freelancer or agency owner to work with. Our local, particularly bilingual Latinas, may be working in PR, but they're not necessarily a top leader or running consultancies. Again, the "why" has perplexed me—particularly given that some of these pros can work in English and Spanish. That should mean double the opportunities, double the money, and double the ganas!

LATINAS: UNDERREPRESENTED IN PR

I became a business owner in 2015, primarily so I could work from home to be closer to my children's school. Working in the demanding PR world, I wanted to remove commuting from my professional scorecard. I wanted to grow as a leader in PR, and I also wanted to play a major role in my kids' lives. Research and conversations have shown me that women, particularly Latinas, may hold themselves back from advancing into leadership roles because of the dueling pressures of personal and professional responsibilities. I understand that reality. As a mom, I also struggle to make it all work well.

In 2024, research on Latinas in PR by Rosalynn A. Vasquez, PhD, and Marlene S. Neill, PhD, APR, Fellow PRSA, shared how mid-management and senior-level Latina PR leaders were faring. Key findings showed that Latinas in PR often face **crucible experiences** or adverse challenges that become critical turning points in their lives. These experiences offered a reflection period in which Latinas assessed the duality of their lives (language, culture, or identities at work versus home) and reexamined their career goals. Because of these hard crucible experiences, these Latina leaders gained confidence, tolerance, and empathy.

Before this study, few Latina participants had been included in publications about women in PR.

The reason for the omission isn't clear. Perhaps previous authors were not connected to Latinas in PR through their network. Perhaps not enough Latinas in PR are known or seen at the leadership level. Regardless of the reason, Latinas should not be missing from important spotlights, particularly in PR where Latina contributions are so badly needed.

According to Pew Research Center, Latinas stand at 22.2 million and account for 17 percent of all adult women in the United States today. This population grew 5.6 million from 2010 to 2022, the largest increase of any major female racial or ethnic group. These numbers underline the gap in PR industry stats and the need to increase Latina representation in PR so Latinas working in PR can increase awareness and interest in the PR field. Many young Latinas have to "see her to be her."

TIME TO REPRESENT

In my experience, Latinas often need extra encouragement to advance themselves. Advancement can come in the form of going after a promotion, asking for a pay increase, or tackling a big goal.

What is the hesitation about? It seems the pressures Latinas face may be uniquely tough—enough to make researchers think of a crucible! We're born into family norms and social scripts about what it means to be "good." A good daughter, sister, wife, and worker. Those measurements are often held against Latinas. Perhaps Latinas are not being encouraged as often to be good leaders—and leaders have to stand out from a group.

Research shows that most Latino families are brought up in a **collectivist culture**, where the needs of the group come before the needs of the individual. This can have positive and negative consequences for Latinas.

In a positive sense, Latinas use collectivist cultural attributes to work well with others and support their connections. In a negative sense, Latinas who think of others' needs first can neglect their own. I have coached several Latinas who are close to their families but sometimes feel limited by these relationships. Their families' opinions or obligations make it hard for these ladies to focus on their college or career goals. Being brought up with collectivist values can also make it harder for Latinas to position themselves to stand out. Most Latinas do not learn how to develop their personal brand and share achievements in the workforce from their family units.

Latinas *do* have influence, particularly within families, but we do not always realize the leverage that offers us. Understanding our **agency**—the innate right to direct our own lives and advocate for ourselves—can help us live more thoughtful lives. Going against different familial and societal pressures or scripts to pave a new path can be lonely at first. Find people who encourage you in healthy ways as you forge ahead.

Since 2020, I've felt emboldened to pursue bigger goals. My goal now is to illustrate possibility and create a clear path for Latinas to follow along with or after me. Before I take a risk, I, too, hear a small inner voice tell me to stop or slow down. Determined to identify that particular type of head trash, I tried to find the right word or saying to best describe that negative self-talk.

I asked some top Latina leaders if they knew which phrase or word I could use to describe the lifelong inner worry that holds Latinas back. Did we not want to be seen as *chiflada* or *necia?* Finding the right term for this kept bothering me. The word had something to do with enoughness. It had something to do with not wanting to be chastised by our families and something to do with the pressure to stay small and accommodating.

Marianismo, a term I first saw used by Latina leadership coach Ruby Garcia, best describes this. According to Verywell Mind, "Marianismo culture encapsulates an idealized traditional feminine gender role characterized by submissiveness, selflessness, chastity, hyper-femininity, and the acceptance of machismo in males."

I've used marianismo in writing and discussions since, but most women I speak with are unfamiliar with it. No matter the term, Latinas must stop driving with their foot on the brake. We slow ourselves down and are overly cautious about switching lanes when it comes to work. The time is now to invite other Latinas into PR and to go after leadership roles in the field. We're worthy of starting consultancies and being top, visible leaders. Let's move from missing in PR to being an essential in PR. You can help spread that message by reading and sharing this book.

RACHEL BENAVIDEZ

———

"The truth is my leap to PR was in large part a leap of faith—faith that I could find my footing, learn fast, and get good before anyone noticed."

Sometimes, big opportunities come in small packages. Mine came wrapped inside a breakfast taco.

I was a cub reporter tasked with covering a breakfast fundraiser at the local high school. It was my chance at a byline for my hometown paper, and a lesson in never saying no to an opportunity—or a taco.

The details about that story have mostly faded, other than it was the humble beginning of my first "real" job. That brief and perhaps overlooked article was the beginning of a career in storytelling and my own story unfolding.

I was born and raised in South Texas, in the shadow of the

United States-Mexico border and the light of a large, loving family who patched me together like a quilt of their collective talents, interests, and aspirations.

As a little girl, I spent hours at the public library, devouring books and encyclopedias. I learned to read my grandmother's novellas *en español,* which she would stuff between the couch cushions for safekeeping. I wrote fairy tales for fun and used big words to impress the adults. I was the kid who had "corrects the teacher too much" written on my report card more than once—like it was a bad thing. Could a career in communications be far behind? Like most good stories, mine had a few twists.

My start in the communications field was on the catching end of story pitches, as a dual language writer and editor. I wasn't raised in public relations (PR). I grew up, so to speak, in the newsroom. Like many reporters starting out, I romanticized the idea of being a member of the press, a profession enshrined in the Constitution—and pop culture.

It was the latter that most inspired me as a young girl.

BECOMING LOIS LATINA

For as long as I can remember, my answer to: "What do you want to be when you grow up?" was invariably: "Lois Lane," the award-winning journalist (and Superman's main squeeze). She was a hero in her own right. She spoke truth to power, and through her reporting, shined a light on people and events that mattered in her world. That's what I wanted to do, though I came to my first newsroom job on a bit of a different path than Lois.

I was a college student when I answered an ad for a job in the newsroom, where I started out typing obituaries and answering phones. My mother had been diagnosed with cancer, and I had been called back home to help while she recovered and continued treatment. She couldn't work for several months, and it fell to me, her only daughter, to care for her and keep the family afloat for a while. That meant holding down three jobs and trying to keep up with my studies, though the urgency of one often outweighed the other.

Weekends were spent behind the counter at my uncle's business. I found a work-study job on campus, and an evening shift at the local paper, where I earned my way to a part-time job on the features desk and was assigned to cover that taco fundraiser for a teacher who had fallen ill. I met another teacher there who later told me about a suspected cancer cluster at the campus. My reporting on that tip led to a state investigation and a large-scale asbestos abatement. Those stories earned me a spot on the news desk. Five years and hundreds of stories later, I became editor-in-chief of that paper.

A friend jokingly called me "Lois Latina." She didn't know how much the comparison meant to the little girl who had just been given her dream job and a modest place in my hometown's history. I was the first woman, the first Latina, and at twenty-seven, the youngest to hold the position in the paper's 111-year history.

A happy side note: my mom recovered from cancer, returned to work, and even returned to school. Over the next few years, I experienced a role reversal. I watched her do her homework at my kitchen table and eventually cross the commencement stage to collect her degree. It was a proud moment for both of us.

BE THE FIRST, BUT NOT THE LAST

As Latinas, we often know the privilege and the challenge of being first. First-born daughters know it especially well. Among my close circle of friends and colleagues, I know Latinas who were the first to go to college, the first to own a home, the first to travel abroad, the first to hold political office, the first to chair a board. I could go on. We are also often the first to raise our hand, the first to help, and the first to reach back.

The privilege of being first is the moment you plant your flag as a pioneer on your respective hilltop. The challenge *and opportunity* are ensuring you aren't the last to reach its summit. It's not just about breaking through ceilings, even the tallest ones. It's also about changing the narrative and pulling down the ladder so others can ascend.

I was at a high point in my own career, part of a team of Latina editors who were directing statewide coverage, when I decided to leave journalism. It wasn't easy. I had to look beyond the horizon at what came next for me and the industry.

The decision came at a time when newsrooms were experiencing a seismic shift that we all saw coming—or should have. Staffs were shrinking. Advertising was drying up. Diversity interests were riding uncomfortably in the back seat. The business model wasn't working, and the job I fell in love with was changing in ways I didn't like.

Those in PR today have seen the outcome of those shifts. It's a different game, and getting coverage for your clients or issues is made more difficult by leaner staffs, earlier deadlines, and a growing focus on clicks. If your news isn't the kind that generates web traffic, likes, or shares, good luck to you, sister.

For me, bringing the viewpoint of a Latina writer and editor with bicultural perspectives and sensitivities was a major plus. Representation matters in all aspects, perhaps especially from a storyteller's vantage point. Having someone who looks or sounds like you, who has experienced life from your perspective, or who sees things from your viewpoint, matters—especially to those watching your footsteps carve out their future paths.

MAMA SAID THERE'D BE DAYS LIKE THESE

My career has existed in markets and regions where Hispanics are the majority. While being Latina didn't make me unique, statistically speaking, it did make me a valuable voice in fields where diversity is still lacking. The truth is, my leap to PR was in large part, a leap of faith—faith that I could find my footing, learn fast, and get good before anyone noticed. My plan then was to leverage my "insider" knowledge in a glamorous PR job. I was half right.

If anyone tells you that PR work isn't hard work, they've never done it. My first year was like drinking from a firehose while learning to drive on the left side of the road. PR introduced me to a new language as well as different ways to look at strategy and to define success.

I landed a leadership role at an impressive local firm known for its brand of Hispanic marketing. Making the switch seemed easy, in theory. If words were my currency, how different could the exchange rate be? The objective was similar enough—get your news out there and make it good. Still, the voice in my head was cautious and doubtful but it was my mother's voice that rang clear.

Whenever I questioned whether I was ready or right for a big step—whether it was trying out for cheerleading in sixth grade or switching careers just before I turned forty—her answer was always, "Of course you are!" Followed by, "And if not, you'll learn."

My mom, though now much changed by age and illness, was also a hero and my prototype for a strong, independent Latina woman. From her, I learned what to and not to do in most scenarios. Do be brave when you must. Don't be careless and get hurt.

She taught herself to drive, made us a home, and herself a career after abandoning her college education because, as a single mother, she had to. She taught us to be relentless and self-sufficient because she knew we would have to one day. And when times got tough, she taught us to rely on each other and accept help because everyone has to, sometimes.

With the confidence my mother gave me, I decided to make a change in search of new growth opportunities that seemed few to non-existent in an industry fighting for survival and, perhaps naively, to achieve something that resembled work-life balance.

Every time I use that phrase, I remember advice from a friend in the tech field, CEO of her own company, and a big deal on several levels. "There is no balance," she said while holding her new baby on her hip and addressing a conference of women leaders, like a boss. "There are only choices. You make them for yourself, and if you don't like the outcome, you make a different choice." It's such simple advice but so true.

FINDING MY 'WHY'

For me, the choice to cross over was not without some bumps. I recall being in a strategy session at the first PR firm I joined after journalism. As we wrapped up, the project leader turned to me in what surely was a test and said, "Rachel, did you get all that?" "I sure did," I answered, perhaps too quickly. Then he asked me to put together "the deck." I was eager to jump in to my first big assignment. I had just one question: "What's a deck?" It was one of many instances I realized there isn't a one-to-one exchange rate when you travel from journalism to PR.

A year into agency work, I had the lingo down, but it became clear something was missing. I thought back to my early career, why I loved it, and the lessons it taught me.

At its heart, public relations work is about making connections through storytelling. Stories people need to know, want to hear, and those that have not yet been told. What drives me is finding a purpose, a connection to the greater good. I knew I wanted to tell stories about struggle and triumph, about service and helping our neighbors, about everyday heroes and happier endings.

I gathered up my courage, summoned my mother's voice, and took another leap, working in the same field but for a public service agency with a mission to connect our community to more opportunities. While there is no superhero equivalent for the PR pro working at a public service entity, there should be. The career journey that started as an idolization of a heroic cartoon newswoman became something quite different. And yet, it remains a core part of why I love what I get to do.

When I officially joined the PR profession, I was, at best, a transplant from a neighboring industry. At worst, I felt like a visitor from another side of town. In time, it became a home. Along the way, I've learned a few things.

I now see my distinct experiences as complementary—two parts of a process aimed at telling stories from valid and unique perspectives. I found new ways to give a voice to the issues and events that shape communities. I figured out how to write my next chapter and decided that if you stay hungry—for wisdom, learning, life, and the occasional taco—every bite tastes like success.

VISIBILITY MOMENT

Twice, I've been written about in my career. Once by a *Texas Monthly* reporter who described me as a "shoo-in for class president" and once by a local women's magazine who said I was "formidable." I can find and appreciate the compliment in each. Most often, I try to find the balance between the two. Lately, I've been examining how those two personas that co-exist even came to be.

Growing up on the Texas-Mexico border in the 1970s and 1980s meant everything had a bicultural existence. Food, family, friends, our language, our history, even our prospects for future success were seen through the lens of a rich culture and sometimes limiting societal views.

Gender norms were fixed and finite, dictating everything from what was appropriate to wear and say, to what life choices were acceptable to pursue and achieve. Humility, deference, and femininity were expected from *niñas buenas* (good girls). A lifetime of learning how to be these things led to some unexpected outcomes that I'm still reconciling. Namely, the reluctance to accept compliments, highlight my own accomplishments, declare my own value, or demand my own worth, at the risk of appearing difficult or *chocante* (conceited).

Here's what I've learned, or un-learned about being "good." It doesn't mean conforming or shrinking to make others comfortable. For me, it means believing in something and advocating for it. Even if that something is only me and my ability to do good in the world. I learned that if we're lucky, we will have people in our life who champion us in rooms we're not always in. But if we're smart, and maybe a little bit brave, we'll learn to do it for ourselves. The confidence to speak positively and knowledgeably about one's own accomplishments can't be discounted on the road to success—whether you are leading others or navigating your own rise.

It took years for me to realize how much growing up a lot Latina and a little Catholic shaped my world-view and self-view.

Knowing why we do what we *do—or don't do*—for ourselves and others can be a lifelong endeavor. Understanding our roots is sometimes required before spreading our wings.

BIOGRAPHY

Rachel Benavidez has experienced communications from both sides of the field, as a writer and editor for newspapers and magazines and a public relations and marketing executive whose work is focused on uplifting communities through storytelling and advocacy.

Her work has included developing messaging and outreach strategies, internal and external communications, thought leadership, branding and marketing campaigns. She also established social responsibility programs that helped amplify that agency's voice and reach and made them key partners in local relief efforts at the height of the COVID-19 pandemic.

Her career includes fifteen years leading newsrooms for English and Spanish publications and award-winning work in journalism, marketing, PR, and digital and social media.

A Rio Grande Valley native, Rachel has spent her life and career in South and Central Texas, telling the stories of the Latino communities she serves. Outside her professional career, she is seated on several boards focused on advancing business and economic development interests, public education and science, technology, engineering and math (STEM) curriculum for girls, and elevating those in the PR industry.

Her work to empower communities in South Texas was presented for discussion at the Barbara Jordan National Forum on Public Policy, and her contributions to the journalism and communications fields have been recognized with numerous local, state, and national awards.

Rachel Benavidez

LinkedIn: Rachel Benavidez

LEADERSHIP IS ESSENTIAL TO PUBLIC RELATIONS

ANAIS BIERA MIRACLE

———

"When you have an engaged leader, you have an engaged workforce. When you have a disengaged leader, you have a disengaged workforce."

The practice of public relations (PR) is one you will master by becoming a tactician and graduating to a strategist, which will take time, experience, and grace. One of the most important aspects of PR is the principle of leadership. In this manuscript, I will share the learnings I have acquired through my nearly two decades of working in the communications field.

CONSEJO

I had the privilege to learn from exceptional leaders, with whom I have acquired new knowledge to utilize as a chief communications officer for one of the largest Latino-led nonprofit organizations in the United States. I would like to impart advice provided by my father, and he told me, *"Mija,* the knowledge you learn should be shared and never kept to oneself, as that does not advance and help others." I have taken that to heart as my father is a person to whom I owe so much, as he has been my role model and someone I strive to be like. It is my responsibility to share the learnings and leadership principles I have received throughout my career and share them with my colleagues, mentees, and those who will be our next generation of communication executive leaders.

When speaking about the fundamentals of leadership in PR, I learned this from my executive coach, Denise Garcia Simpson, PhD, founder of the Masters of Leadership Institute. She said, "When emotions are high, logic is low." In the arena of crisis communications, in which I have extensive experience, "when emotions are high, logic is low" is the core of what we, as communications practitioners, are trained for. That is to be calm in the eye of the storm. Chaos may ensue around you; however, you need to tune out the rumors, chatter, and even internal negative self-talk and focus on getting the information culled and accurate. You must communicate clearly, consistently, and compassionately because there is no room for error during a crisis.

Over the course of the summer semester while in my

Executive Master of Public Leadership program at the University of Texas at Austin's LBJ School of Public Affairs, I have come to the following personal conclusion: Executives are hired for their subject matter expertise, but most critically, how they handle a crisis. Leaders must master emotional intelligence and build trust with their teams, departments, and organizations. They should lead with compassion, transparency, integrity, and resolve.

ENGAGED LEADERSHIP

A more recent occurrence with managing social media was the proliferation of disinformation. As a result of disinformation, our organization was dealing with vitriolic social media rants, foul-language laced emails, and voicemail messages that were borderline terroristic. While that was going on from August 2023 to late 2024, we listened to social media conspiracy theorists and poured over their inflammatory rhetoric, which can take an emotional and mental toll on one's well-being. I decided it would be best for us to take what we learned through this social media disinformation situation, read the book, *On Disinformation: How to Fight for Truth and Protect Democracy* by Lee McIntyre, and train frontline staff in the field. Staff are the first line of defense when caring for a vulnerable population, such as children and youth.

Instead of creating the training online and having staff watch me and the director of media relations and multimedia talk about what to do and not do when engaging with social media activists and media, we were in the field training staff. When you have an engaged leader, you have an engaged workforce. When you have a disengaged leader, you have a disengaged workforce. Leaders must be comfortable not just delegating what needs to be implemented but be prepared to be in the field to meet the teams where they are. There can be a disconnect and perception that leadership is removed from what happens daily in the field, when making decisions, and not considering feedback from the staff doing the work. However, you must consider that each scenario must be assessed on a case-by-case basis to make the proper decision that is in the best interest of the organization. And at times, you may have to make a unilateral decision.

A further example of engaged leadership is when, around 2022, I took a tour of our programs throughout Texas, California, and Arizona to conduct communication focus groups with frontline staff from first, second, third, and weekend shifts. It was a humbling experience to hear from staff members who shared their experiences on how we could improve communications from the field to corporate headquarters.

As a result of conducting countless focus groups, staff would even share they were here to bring their concerns to the forefront for staff who either were on the floor and could not attend, or were advocating on their behalf. As a result of my experience, I decided to hire a first-of-its-kind internal communications position for this specific division. The person I hired came from the field, had compliance experience, and understands the voice of the employees who work directly with the youth we serve matters.

I then subsequently hired an internal communications manager for the region that covers Arizona and California, and this was because we needed direct staff in the field. I would not have had that information had I not been in the field and requested team members to share their communication needs with me.

THE 1 PERCENT

As a former chief public relations officer and now a chief communications officer, I represent the "1 percent of C-suite executives (who) are Latina," according to the article "Latinas Are Ambitious but Least Represented Group in the C-Suite" by Holly Corbett, published by Forbes on June 14, 2024. We must make strides to break the glass ceiling and increase the percentage of Latinas who occupy the C-suite. As a chief, it is my duty to ensure we create succession planning to cultivate the next generation of C-suite executives, leaders, and individual star performers. To increase the number of Latinas in C-suite executive positions, we must coach and mentor Latinas, when we see their professional and educational potential and capacity. Additionally, taking time to inquire about their professional aspirations, and how we may support their endeavors to achieve their goals will set them on a path to realize their utmost potential.

Most importantly, we must invite those we see as having incredible potential and plant the seed from within that they can achieve greatness. At times, colleagues may feel compelled to take the next steps to reach their aspirations but may not know how to take the next strategic risk. I have learned from Dr. Simpson that we can either be risk averse or risk tolerant—and trust me, it can be daunting to make a considerable change that impacts your life, and those around you, such as your immediate family.

HUMANIZING LEADERSHIP

When leading a team, we must humanize leadership. We have families, loved and cherished ones, and many of us contribute outside of our careers, such as serving on board of directors, volunteering, furthering our education, etc. As a leader, if you expect your team to go above and beyond, you must demonstrate this very attribute. Also, as a leader, remember we are human. I cannot expect a team member to give 100 percent of themselves if they are preoccupied with pressing issues relating to their immediate family, loved ones, illness, and other variables out of our control. What I can do is be compassionate, be an active listener, and ask what I may do for them in their time of need.

While pursuing my master's in public leadership at University of Texas at Austin, one of my instructors was retired Lieutenant General William Troy, US Army, who said the one attribute leaders have, which transcends other characteristics, was the practice of caring. This I find is accurate. If you demonstrate caring to those you lead, it has been my experience this creates a positive dynamic within the team.

Lastly, trust is essential for effective leadership. You must build authentic and intentional working relationships to build a cohesive and collaborative team. An excellent book that outlines this and should be read by leaders is Patrick Lencioni's *The Five Dysfunctions of a Team.*

PAVING OUR OWN PATH

As Latinas, we must seek opportunities to advance our professional careers, such as investing in advanced degrees, pursuing continuous professional development, seeking executive coaching, and taking strategic risks. There are times we may need to be invited to the table to consider a professional opportunity. For example, Melissa Vela-Williamson has been my friend and professional mentor for almost as long as I have been in the field of PR. Melissa reached out to me in 2021 after learning of an opportunity in Austin, that she said I should consider applying. I remember reading the qualifications and thought to myself, I do not know if I should apply. Melissa sent an email to me and the individual seeking an applicant for the position, and the rest is history.

At times, we must chart our own path, even though that road was never paved for us. We may proceed with caution and embrace the adventure and opportunity that may open doors for us that may never have existed if we had traversed lightly or not at all. Everything we do is a risk. Why not take a strategic risk? Consider being risk-tolerant the next time you are asked to take on a position that may take you beyond your comfortability. We may not realize we can achieve greatness unless we get out of our own way to manifest our brilliance.

VISIBILITY MOMENT

I realized in my twenty-year career in PR that my role as a tactician and strategist culminated in my expertise in crisis communications. After handling a crisis at my previous employer and finding I could tolerate the 24/7 mentality, managing emotions, communicating internally with staff and externally with media, and being part of a litigation team, I found my calling. I have embodied the "when emotions are high, logic is low" mentality. I find when working in a crisis, I leverage my expertise and learnings in leadership. PR professionals who work in crisis communications management have a refined skillset that involves leadership, psychology, communications, and emotional intelligence. I found my passion first-hand via direct experience, which is a great teacher.

Crisis communications may not be for all; but as a chief communications officer, this is one of the most important practices of our times. We are working within evolving landscapes of technology, the viral spread of disinformation, 24/7 media consumption, and the proliferation of cybersecurity threats. To prepare to handle a crisis, write a crisis communications plan, and read *The Prepared Leader* by Erika H. James and Lynn Perry Wooten.

BIOGRAPHY

Anais Biera Miracle has two decades of public relations and nonprofit leadership experience. Anais is the Chief Communications Officer for one of the largest, Latino-led nonprofits in the United States. Anais specializes in crisis communications and litigation public relations.

She was the chief public relations officer for a nonprofit in San Antonio for nearly twelve years, where she led communications and advocacy on behalf of youth and families involved in the Texas foster care system.

Anais has a bachelor of arts degree in political science from the University of the Incarnate Word and is a graduate of the San Antonio Hispanic Chamber of Commerce Alex Briseño Leadership Development Program and Latina Leadership Institute, Leadership Austin Essential Class 45, and various leadership programs. Anais is pursuing her master's degree in public leadership from the University of Texas at Austin's Lyndon B. Johnson School of Public Affairs.

Anais received the Image de San Antonio Award as an Outstanding Hispanic Woman Role Model, the Yellow Rose of Texas Award through the Office of the Governor, recognizing women for their contributions to their communities and the state of Texas, and the Del Oro Community Service Award from the Public Relations Society of America San Antonio Chapter.

Anais is married and has a daughter, and is the daughter of Gilberto Biera, Jr., and Mary Helen Biera of Castroville, Texas.

Anais Biera Miracle

LinkedIn: Anais Biera Miracle

PROPELLED BEYOND CONVENTIONAL PR BOUNDARIES

CARMEN BOON, MA

"A deep appreciation for cultural sensitivity has taught me that a career in PR and communications is a life commitment to understand and respect people from all walks of life."

I hail from southern Venezuela, where industrial towns intersect with the vast jungles at the edge of the Amazon Basin. My father, who emigrated from Colombia as the descendant of a Lebanese immigrant family, moved to Venezuela in the 1960s following a call for physicians to assist people in remote and impoverished towns. It was in one of these rural hospitals that he met my mother, an aspiring nurse. They embarked on their journey together, raising four children among rich rainforests, stunning waterfalls, and bustling factories—elements that profoundly influenced my views on labor and life. The straightforwardness, simplicity, and endurance of our local communities instilled in me essential lessons about hard work and adaptability early on. My academic path was also impacted by the Jesuit ethos that promotes a holistic approach to education that nurtures intellectual growth alongside moral and social responsibility. These principles provided me with a lifelong commitment to justice, ethics, and service.

A year after I graduated from high school, I moved to Caracas to pursue a bachelor's degree in journalism at Universidad Católica Andres Bello, a renowned Jesuit institution. After much deliberation, my decision to pursue this career was fueled by a desire to understand and articulate the complex social dynamics of my country through media narratives. The city's vibrant culture, economic contrasts, and dynamic media landscape made it an ideal backdrop for my early academic and career endeavors.

Journalism school exceeded all my expectations. It offered a portal to the world, a collaborative space for exchanging views on politics, history, social issues, and the arts, lasting collegiality and friendships, and a hub for developing projects centered around media theory and hands-on media making. I seized every chance to engage in internships, field trips, hands-on training, and teaching assistant roles. Beyond the confines of the university, I fully absorbed the social and cultural vibrancy that Caracas had to offer at that time as fuel for my communications career.

Reflecting on my beginnings as a communicator, I initially

felt I had no mentors. However, further introspection made me realize the influence several women in communications had on my career, often in ways I hadn't fully recognized at the time. Two experiences, in particular, stand out.

In my early twenties in Venezuela, I landed a real job as a public relations (PR) coordinator at a well-known cultural institution before even finishing college. I attribute this stroke of luck to serendipitously meeting the head of that communications department, Gisela Gil, a talented communicator who had an unparalleled ability to lead but also create a familial atmosphere in the workplace. Gisela possessed a personal magnetism and zest for life, often leading our team to enjoy long and splendid lunches together outside the office, silently hopeful that we would be working late that night, enjoying each other's company.

She was an incredible connector, forging meaningful relationships both professionally and personally. Her down-to-earth, no-nonsense communication style was paired with a special talent for making our writing not only accurate but also compelling. Gisela was the first to debunk myths about argument and persuasion for me, shaping my approach as a PR and media relations professional. Despite being only a few years older than the rest of us, she was a true mama bear, teaching us invaluable lessons about loyalty and genuine support.

At my second and my first post-college job, I was a junior reporter at a national newspaper. Facing intense scrutiny from my male supervisor, I was eventually let go. At twenty-four, this experience left me feeling devastated and ashamed.

Determined to change the course of events, I contacted my small professional network for advice, including my boss at the cultural institution. Through these conversations, Gisela connected me with a group of accomplished women in a PR agency, ultimately leading me to a corporate communications role within a team helmed by another incredible female boss, Ingrid Priego. Although this job diverged from my early aspirations as a budding journalist eager to report breaking news and connect with a wide audience, it proved to be an invaluable experience that emphasized the importance of staying adaptable and offered significant opportunities for personal and professional development. This she boss also played an instrumental role in guiding me through this difficult transition. Ingrid entrusted me with interesting projects and involved me in various company employee affinity groups.

Motivated by a belief that global perspectives are essential for impactful storytelling, a year after graduating from journalism school, I applied for a US Fulbright grant to further my studies in journalism and media in the United States. Receiving the grant a year later was a moment of immense pride.

When I informed Ingrid of this news, she hugged me tightly, expressed genuine happiness for my achievement, and later organized a grand farewell party with goodie bags and delicious food. Throughout that day, I was touched by the overwhelming support from these female colleagues. A few months later, filled with gratitude and free from resentment toward my previous employers, I set off for the United States.

Paradoxically, these two women untimely left this world under different tragic circumstances, solidifying my belief that perhaps they were here to show many how to live and work.

REJECTION LEADING TO REINVENTION

I had a privileged position during my first two years in the United States as a Fulbright student. Though my stipend afforded me a frugal lifestyle, I was immersed in everything I could desire—an exciting master's program, a community composed of academics, and students from across the US and around the globe, and the vibrant city of New York.

Breaking into the fiercely competitive media and communications job market in New York City (NYC) without any professional connections was a huge challenge. Confronting a barrage of rejections for roles in PR and journalism at agencies and media outlets in the city, largely due to my non-traditional experience and the complications of visa sponsorship, I was prompted to reinvent myself.

During this transitional period, I realized that my college education in journalism could be a significant asset and that my aspirations in journalism could be effectively channeled into a niche within in-house PR and communications. The skills I had sharpened such as research, writing, and critical thinking were highly transferable. My ability to dig deep into stories, see the big picture, ask the right questions, and present information clearly and compellingly could enhance my effectiveness in this area. In addition, my proficiency in Spanish and understanding of the Hispanic community proved to be assets in my job search.

My perspective as the first and only in my family to immigrate from a politically volatile country equipped me to tackle communications projects with a deeper awareness of potential barriers. I always pose critical questions to myself and everyone working with me: Can this message be easily comprehended by families spanning multiple generations? Is the language straightforward and accessible to everyone? Are our translations not only precise but also culturally resonant? Are we ensuring materials are available in all languages spoken by the communities we aim to serve? Are our examples and talking points respectful and pertinent to our target cultural group or audience?

In addition to this, deep appreciation for cultural sensitivity compels me to ensure that every communications piece is not only technically accurate but also empathetically designed to meet the diverse needs of the communities we serve. It has also taught me that a career in PR and communications goes beyond being just a job. It is a life commitment to understand and respect people from all walks of life.

LATINA IDENTITY AS AN ASSET AND A RESPONSIBILITY

Embracing my Latina identity in the realm of public service and outreach has not merely been an asset but also a responsibility.

My direct experiences with the intricate US immigration system have given me a unique insight into the hurdles faced by new Hispanic immigrants, especially regarding misconceptions about their identity as Latinx individuals. A persistent mistake in the news media is the inclination to view our communities as culturally uniform. This oversimplification not only undermines the richness and diversity of our cultures but also comes across as insensitive.

In my roles within the NYC government and nonprofit communications sector, I have been fortunate to help enable access to vital services for Spanish-speaking populations, including initiatives like the affordable housing lottery, reliable healthcare access, and seeking justice through sexual harassment discrimination claims in the workplace. My growing understanding of these communities' linguistic and cultural barriers motivated me more and more to think carefully about targeted outreach plans to enhance their access to opportunities.

Developing requests for proposals to engage Latino-led minority and women-owned marketing and PR businesses and spearheading crucial citywide campaigns—such as the FEMA-funded outreach involving Latino influencers for COVID-19 testing—are further examples of how my cultural insights in the public sector have been crucial in reaching and positively impacting hard-to-reach Spanish-speaking communities and ensuring that their voices are heard, respected, and empowered.

ADVOCATING FOR BILINGUALISM WITH AN ACCENT

Being bilingual is an incredible asset, and it's something to be embraced fully in our careers. Not only has a career in government communications allowed me to break communication barriers within essential government programs, but it also enabled me to craft messages that deeply resonated with Spanish-speaking communities, mobilizing them into action.

However, getting to this realization was far from easy. Languages don't come naturally to me, and it took immense effort to achieve a decent Test of English as a Foreign Language (TOEFL) score to gain admission to colleges in the United States. The excitement of moving to NYC quickly gave way to some difficult realities I faced. In college, I grappled with the courage to speak up in class, articulate my thoughts clearly, and ensure I was understood. Writing in English posed an even greater challenge; my papers took me three to four times longer to complete compared to my peers. Completing my thesis was a monumental task, and I often joke that it prematurely gave me white hair and wrinkles in my late twenties.

Getting a job in the Venezuelan Consulate in NYC and its mission to the United Nations was a turning point in which I truly recognized and put into practice the power of bilingualism. This was a predominantly Spanish-speaking environment where I was one of the few fluent in English.

Navigating the obstacles and misunderstandings tied to my

accent, which is an essential element of my bilingual identity, has also proved challenging. At first, I strongly perceived that some colleagues equated my accent with poor English skills, overlooking me for jobs and projects. Yet, I embraced this difference as a source of empowerment.

In my early career days in NYC, I eagerly volunteered for opportunities to present at internal meetings and represent my organization at various speaking events, including engaging with English media. By doing so, I believe I've contributed to a shift in perception, allowing others to see and hear voices that sound like mine. Despite being in such a diverse city, I often found myself as the sole Spanish speaker in many meetings and events. I embraced this opportunity offering my translation skills to bridge communication gaps. By advocating for the translation of materials into Spanish, some of which had never been available in the language before, I also played a role in fostering inclusivity and broadening the reach of my organization's message.

Through these simple actions, I underscored the value of bilingualism as a strategic asset and cultivated more welcoming work environments, slowly transforming viewpoints and demonstrating how bilingualism and having an accent can be powerful tools for connection and understanding.

EMBRACING MY SECOND ACT

The most valuable lesson and the greatest opportunity I've encountered is intentionally defining and embracing my second act. In my twenty-plus years of experience, I've developed and executed large-scale, issue-focused campaigns that have not only shaped public opinion but also influenced policy decisions and generated revenue for governmental and non-profit initiatives. In a world where the importance of policy communications is skyrocketing, I'm excited to continue leading the charge in a field where I can blend my passion for storytelling with my ability to navigate the intricate landscape of public policy. One of my main goals for the remainder of my professional career is to demystify policy for others and make it accessible, engaging, and effective by crafting campaigns that resonate across the public, nonprofit, and private sectors.

Outside of work, I have been engaging in activities I once deemed unnecessary or too time-consuming. One of the most transformative of these activities has been joining women in communications and PR networking groups. The catalyst for this move was a series of toxic work environments that pushed me to a breaking point. Seeking solace and support, I found these groups to be a unique source of encouragement.

By engaging with these networks, I've refined my approach to networking and fostered a stronger sense of community. Exchanging experiences, providing support, and empowering other women in communications have driven me forward more significantly than in the past twenty years, ultimately leading me to a greater sense of peace and fulfillment.

VISIBILITY MOMENT

I am convinced that fostering strong interpersonal connections is key to implementing effective PR and communications campaigns that serve everyone's interests. In the world of PR, developing solid ties with team members, colleagues from other departments, clients, and other stakeholders reflects on impactful work that reaches and benefits broader audiences.

BIOGRAPHY

Carmen Boon serves as the Vice President for Public Affairs at Food Bank For New York City. With over two decades of experience, Carmen is distinguished for crafting strategic communications plans and orchestrating large-scale, issue-focused, multi-platform, multicultural, and multilingual public affairs and integrated media campaigns that have significantly heightened awareness for governmental and nonprofit initiatives, influenced policy, shaped public opinion, and generated both public and private revenue.

Before her current role, Carmen spent fifteen years in various capacities within NYC government agencies. During her public service tenure, she tackled outreach challenges related to housing shortages, essential social services delivery, worker and immigrant rights advocacy, and critical public health enhancements. As part of the city's senior press corps, she adeptly navigated crisis communications plans during economic recessions, natural disasters, and public health crises.

Carmen's work has been recognized by the Women Changing the World Awards, Shorty Awards, MarCom Awards, PRWeek Purpose Awards, and AVA Digital Awards. She is a board member for the NY Greater Chapter of the Fulbright Association and an active member of CHIEF, the Public Relations Society of America, 100 Hispanic Women, the Association of Latino Professionals for America, and Feeding America's Policy Engagement and Advocacy Committee.

Originally from Venezuela, Carmen came to the US as a Fulbright scholar. She holds a master of arts degree in media studies from The New School in Manhattan and a journalism degree from Universidad Católica Andrés Bello in Caracas. She currently balances her professional life between NYC and Verona, New Jersey, where she lives with her husband Dan, son Simon, and furry daughter Callista.

Carmen Boon, MA
LinkedIn: Carmen Boon

JILL CASEY PINTOR

"My whole life has been a lesson in accomplishing the impossible. Statistically speaking, I wasn't supposed to succeed."

The opportunity to share my story came at a pivotal point in my career and in my life. I had just lost my mother after her long and courageous fight against a relentless series of medical setbacks. She had a zest for life and fiercely fought to maintain her independence. When she could no longer manage to live alone, I moved her into my home, where I cared for her hands-on and assumed responsibility for her personal affairs, while simultaneously managing my own household, personal, and career obligations. I don't know how I made it through that grueling period, but in retrospect, I wouldn't change a thing.

AGAINST THE ODDS: A JOURNEY OF DETERMINATION

My whole life has been a lesson in accomplishing the impossible. Statistically speaking, I wasn't supposed to succeed. But I refused to become a statistic.

Several studies have shown that Latinas spend more time than their male partners on household activities and caring for family members. When you factor in a profession like PR, where the hours are long and oftentimes unpredictable, it's no surprise that there are so few Latinas in PR. It's a female-dominated industry, but according to a *Data USA Report*,[1] only 12.6 percent of PR professionals are Hispanic.

I was fortunate to have my husband's support, but nonetheless, it was an unrelenting experience. Like so many others, I worked long hours, with days and nights frequently blurring together. I loved my job and worked extremely hard to get where I was. Giving up wasn't an option, so I channeled my mother's indomitable spirit, with a fierce commitment to persevering.

Immediately after the funeral, I immersed myself in my career like never before, while continuing to manage the relentless flow of my mother's lingering final affairs. I was physically, mentally, and emotionally depleted. But life's demands don't subside simply because you are dealing with adversity.

At the time, I was serving as ethics chair on the Public Relations Society of America (PRSA) Southern Arizona Chapter board of directors. One of my responsibilities was to

[1] Data USA, 2022. https://datausa.io/profile/soc/public-relations-specialists#demographics.

deliver an Ethics Month event. As chance would have it, the date I had selected months prior wound up being mere weeks after my mother's passing. I was drained, but PRSA was important to me, and with the help of my fellow board members, I delivered a successful event.

I remained on the board for an additional year. And I'm glad I did because PRSA would later become a guiding light as my career path began to veer in a new direction. I'll share more on that later.

FROM COMMUNITY COLLEGE TO CORPORATE LEADERSHIP

I was first introduced to PR at a high school career day. I was intrigued by the opportunity to be a champion for worthy brands and a source of truth for the media and other stakeholders. Growing up in a small town, the thought of attending a large university right out of high school was intimidating. Besides, I was born into a family of modest financial means and didn't have much money saved up to fund my education. So, I enrolled in Pima Community College (PCC) in Tucson, Arizona, and got a restaurant job to pay for tuition and living expenses. I relied on public transportation and the kindness of my roommates and friends to help me get to and from work and school.

While I didn't realize it at the time, statistically speaking, the odds were against me. A study released in 2024 [2] found that only

[2] Velasco, Tatiana; Fink, John; Bedoya-Guevara, Mariel; Jenkins, Davis; and LaViolet, Tania. "Tracking Transfer: Community College and Four-Year Institutional Effectiveness in Broadening Bachelor's Degree Attainment." Community College Research Center at Teachers College, Columbia University; the Aspen Institute College Excellence Program; and the National Student Clearinghouse Research Center, February 2024. https://ccrc.tc.columbia.edu/publications/Tracking-Transfer-Community-College-and-Four-Year-Institutional-Effectiveness-in-Broadening-Bachelors-Degree-Attainment.html.

sixteen percent of Arizona community college transfer students go on to earn a bachelor's degree within six years of first enrolling in college. The rate drops to thirteen percent for Hispanics.

I was also adversely impacted by the socioeconomic achievement gap, which is twenty-five percent Hispanic and includes children from families living below the federal poverty level, with the highest poverty rates in mother-only households like mine. This was revealed in the *Ballard Brief*.[3]

Perhaps the credit goes to PCC for having a successful transfer program, or maybe it was my tenacity. While I don't have a definitive answer, it didn't hurt that I had a bit of a chip on my shoulder, which I leveraged for motivation.

Unphased by the statistical barriers to my success, I was ambitious and fearless in my youth. I beat the odds and earned my bachelor's degree in only five years while working full-time and completing an internship at a PR firm during my senior year. There, I developed a knack for writing solid press releases and successfully pitching stories to national publications. That evolved into my first "real" full-time job, where I gained both PR and leadership experience from overseeing the internship program. It was a rewarding opportunity. But it was hard to live off the entry-level salary. To earn a little extra money, I continued bartending evenings and weekends at the same restaurant where I worked while attending college.

---

[3] Bradley, Kate (2022) "The Socioeconomic Achievement Gap in the US Public Schools," Ballard Brief: Vol. 2022: Issue 3, Article 10. https://scholarsarchive.byu.edu/ballardbrief/vol2022/iss3/10.

DEFENDING MY IDENTITY AND DEBUNKING ASSUMPTIONS

One day, while searching for client press clippings in the local newspaper, I stumbled upon a job posting for a director of promotions role at the local Telemundo station. I applied and was hired. Initially, I got a few questions about my background. I wasn't surprised. When I was a child, my grandfather nicknamed me "La Gringa," due to my fair skin color.

I momentarily had flashbacks of having been bullied in elementary school for not being "Hispanic enough." I was presumed to be wealthy and ironically labeled a "rich little white girl." The bullies said that I didn't belong at a school comprised of predominantly lower-income Hispanic students. I tried to brush it off, knowing their assumptions couldn't have been further from the truth. But deep down inside, it hurt. And it made me question my identity at the time.

The people at Telemundo were warm, caring and supportive. They even patiently helped me brush up on my Spanish. Growing up on the border and in a Hispanic household, I spoke the language conversationally, although I hadn't spoken it much formally, because when I was growing up, the schools had an English-only mandate. But it wasn't long before I blended seamlessly into the familiar cultural nuances. I felt right at home and earned the nicknames *Güerita* and *Jilita* because the name Jill doesn't exactly translate to Spanish.

One of my favorite projects of my entire career was promoting and facilitating a bilingual (Spanish/English) press conference for a defending champion boxer in a title fight. I also enjoyed meeting Vicente Fernández, Maná and many Mexican celebrities. Every day, I interacted with fascinating guests we featured on a magazine-style TV program, *Encuentro con Tucson*, which I co-produced.

Throughout my career, I had the good fortune of working with many leaders who recognized my hard work and, through words of encouragement, inspired me to always aim higher. One example was a former CEO who dubbed me Rookie of the Year for generating an unprecedented amount of media attention. I'm pretty sure I doubled the coverage the following year.

I spent most of my working years at Vantage West Credit Union. I wound up there after a stroke of bad luck, followed by a silver lining. A change in ownership at my previous employer had resulted in layoffs across the entire management team. That was shortly after 9/11, when the economy was turbulent, and unemployment rates were rising. After nearly four months of fruitlessly searching for a PR job, I had just about given up. Desperately needing to bring in some income, I had gotten licensed to sell pre-need funeral services.

Just as I was about to start cold calling, I got a tip from a former colleague who had recently accepted an executive role at DM Federal Credit Union (known today as Vantage West). They were hiring a marketing specialist. Although I was technically overqualified for the job, I applied and was grateful for the opportunity.

When the hiring manager called me with the good news, he

shared that one of my references, the legendary Raul E. Aguirre, a distinguished figure in the Latino community, had provided a solid recommendation. I knew him from my Telemundo days. He shared that I was uniquely qualified for the role because I grew up on the border (of Agua Prieta, Sonora, Mexico, and Douglas, Arizona, USA). He said that anyone with a background like mine had grit, was used to hard work, and could excel at anything! He was right. My solid work ethic and loyalty earned me several promotions, ultimately leading to the position of vice president of corporate and member communications.

I was incredibly proud of all I had accomplished. Originally hired to help launch an investment services subsidiary, I went on to introduce digital marketing, start a corporate communications division and activate the company's first social media feeds. I also established the foundation for a Hispanic marketing initiative emphasizing cultural integration and celebrating diversity within the various Hispanic market segments. I was looking forward to working on the project. Unfortunately, I was also managing many other priorities and couldn't give the initiative my full focus. But I hired a talented intern who was pursuing his master of business administration (MBA). He delivered a solid pilot program and solidified the launch.

I took great pride in my work at the credit union and looked forward to ending my career there. But headlines of layoffs and company downsizing began to dominate newsfeeds. In an unprecedented move, the credit union introduced a voluntary early retirement option for qualified employees, including me. I had a BIG decision to make.

TURNING TRIALS INTO TRIUMPHS: A LEAP OF FAITH

My first instinct was to stay. After all, there were many exciting initiatives on the horizon that I looked forward to seeing through to fruition. On the other hand, I welcomed the opportunity to exhale, disconnect, and take a desperately needed break.

After deep reflection and a late-evening conversation with my financial advisor, I decided to take a leap of faith. I announced my news via LinkedIn on February 29 (leap day). They say you can tell whether you made the right decision by how you feel the following day. I woke up without a doubt in my mind that I had. It was an opportunity to hit the refresh button, and I welcomed the pivot.

The first few weeks were like a whirlwind and felt somewhat surreal. I spent most of my time tending to unfinished business that I hadn't been able to handle amidst all my other obligations. I also experienced somewhat of an identity crisis. I had nearly forgotten who I was before the relentlessly brutal years of working triple duty as a caretaker, wife and dedicated employee. I had been "on call" 24/7 for either work or caretaking obligations for so long that I found it difficult to shift focus to my next career move.

But I had to start somewhere, so I began funneling through my old work files that overflowed with relics of my past career successes. They were stuffed with old press releases, newspaper clippings and articles I had written. This exercise was a therapeutic walk down memory lane. It amplified my sense of accomplishment and reminded me of my capabilities. I quickly began to channel the tenacious go-getter I was at the onset of my career. I thought about my humble beginnings as a determined high school graduate who worked two summer jobs to save money for school. I recalled the day I left for college on a Greyhound bus with all my belongings in a plastic trash bag to pursue my PR dream.

I was reassured, knowing I had an entire network of PRSA contacts I could lean on as I contemplated my future. That's how I learned of this opportunity to share my story. As I contemplated my next steps, I knew that no matter where I landed, I had already accomplished enough to make myself proud. My diligent attention to financial planning also afforded me the opportunity to take my time determining my next career move.

My whole life was a lesson in accomplishing the impossible. Statistically speaking, I wasn't supposed to succeed. But I already have. And I'm not finished yet.

VISIBILITY MOMENT

I chose a career in PR because I feel fulfilled when I successfully amplify the voices and accomplishments of those I proudly represent. But I've learned that if you don't acknowledge your achievements, you risk having them vanish from history. In observing some of the many well-respected PR practitioners who have mastered the art of gracefully shining the spotlight on themselves, I've come to realize the importance of doing the same, no matter how uncomfortable it might be.

My contribution to this anthology was fueled by my desire to celebrate and memorialize some of the pivotal moments that impacted my career trajectory. While I have won various awards throughout my career, my biggest accomplishment, by far, has been my victory over my circumstances. The key to my success has been a mindset of refusing to let statistics or any other force hinder my potential to succeed.

I hope my story will inspire others who might otherwise be discouraged by obstacles or circumstances that seem impossible to overcome.

BIOGRAPHY

Jill Casey Pintor's communications career spans more than two decades across several industries, including television, entertainment, nonprofits, and finance. Her areas of expertise include corporate communications, brand management, internal communications, media relations, crisis communications, and content writing.

Jill spent much of her career working for Vantage West, one of Southern Arizona's largest credit unions. There, she held several roles with progressively more responsibility, including vice president of corporate and member communications. During her tenure there, Jill helped launch an investment services subsidiary. She also led the credit union's early digital marketing and social media efforts, formed an internal communications division, and laid the foundation for a Hispanic marketing initiative.

After two decades with the credit union, Jill took a leap of faith and pivoted to pursue her passion for writing. That landed her at StreetCred PR, where she accepted a role as a financial content writer.

Earlier in her career, Jill worked for Telemundo, Old Tucson Studios, United Way of Tucson and Southern Arizona, and C.J. Heileman & Associates.

Jill is an Arizona native. She was raised in Douglas and resides in Tucson. She holds a bachelor's degree in communication from the University of Arizona. She is an active member of PRSA's Southern Arizona Chapter and has served three terms as ethics chair.

Jill Casey Pintor

LinkedIn: Jill Casey Pintor

AN ONGOING EVOLUTION AND THE POWER OF WORDS

LILLY CORTÉS WYATT

———————

"I envision a world where diversity is not only embraced but also celebrated, where our differences and individual strengths are valued."

NI DE AQUÍ, NI DE ALLÁ

Growing up between Mexico and the United States, I often felt like La India Maria, a fictional comedic character portrayed by actress María Elena Velasco who often said, *"Yo no soy ni de aquí, ni de allá,"* meaning she didn't feel like she belonged anywhere. I struggled for years with the feeling of not really fitting into either culture. My prominent Spanish accent still leads people to question where I'm from, even though I was born and have lived in the United States for most of my life. It's funny that I chose the field of communication as my career, but I have been in love with it for as long as I can remember.

Over the past few years, I've come to understand and deeply value the significance of diversity. Through my personal experiences, I have gained a profound appreciation for the incredible range of diversity within the Hispanic culture and the broader human community. This diversity isn't limited to just physical traits; it encompasses diverse perspectives, life journeys, and fundamental values, all of which contribute to the richness of our society.

THE SEEDS OF A DREAM

I entered the world in the charming town of Martinez, California, nestled in the beautiful San Francisco Bay Area. At the age of six, my family and I embarked on an exciting journey, moving to the lively and bustling Mexico City, the capital of Mexico. My formative years were a whirlwind of adventures in vibrant cities such as Mexico City, Guadalajara, and Morelia.

As a child in Mexico, while my parents watched the news and my siblings played, I would skip playtime to spend countless hours captivated by the authoritative delivery of national news by Jacobo Zabludovsky, a renowned anchorman. These experiences kindled a deep passion for pursuing a career as a news reporter and working in communications. I dreamt of being a courageous frontline reporter, fearlessly covering wars, apocalyptic scenes, breaking news, and natural disasters. I aspired to share powerful stories of survival and resilience with the world.

In 1993, my family and I moved from the beautiful capital of Michoacan to Pittsburg, California, part of the San Francisco Bay Area. Despite starting at the local high school midway through my junior year, I was excited to discover that the school had a student newspaper. I was eager to write and share stories about my classmates, their achievements, and the latest news and events happening in the school. This opportunity continued to spark my interest in pursuing a career in journalism.

When we moved back to the United States, we envisioned living in a city like those we saw on television, such as *Beverly Hills, 90210*, or *The Wonder Years*, but it was different—oh, so different. Pittsburg had a high minority population—primarily working families of Mexican and Black descent without much generational wealth. For the first time in my life, I witnessed how much of a trap gangs can be for people and the limiting beliefs they impose on those around them. I couldn't help but notice and reflect on the profound sadness that enveloped "that world." I was determined to create a distinctive life for myself. At sixteen, I became acutely aware of the multitude of perspectives and realities that exist in the world, each contributing to our uniqueness.

While writing for my high school newspaper, I discovered Barbara Walters and Oprah Winfrey, and I became determined to pursue a career in journalism and follow in their footsteps. I was especially captivated by Barbara and her exceptional ability to interview and draw out information from anyone. She was so confident, even while interviewing dictators and criminals, and she had incredible charisma and directness that I continue to admire. I wanted to become a journalist and follow in their footsteps.

A powerful experience from my senior year still inspires me. When I sought guidance from our school counselor about college opportunities, I was disheartened by her dismissal of my aspirations, as she mentioned a harmful stereotype about young Latinas—that I would end up pregnant. Although her words lingered in my mind, they also fueled my determination to prove her wrong. My dream of becoming a journalist was unwavering, and I was resolved to pursue it, filled with confidence in my abilities and potential.

THE PATH TO HIGHER EDUCATION

Despite my dream of attending USC's Annenberg School of Journalism, financial constraints and my lack of knowledge about student loans presented challenges I couldn't overcome. Instead, I enrolled at Diablo Valley College (DVC), a community college in Pleasant Hill, California. This choice allowed me to work and study simultaneously. I am still a strong advocate for community colleges because they empower young people, offer affordable tuition, and provide the same high-quality education for general education courses as four-year colleges. I met many great people at DVC, some of whom are still my friends! While there, I earned associate degrees in theater arts and general education while working part-time to save for my bachelor's degree. I seized every opportunity, knowing each step was integral to my journey.

I was accepted at the University of California Davis and San Francisco State University, but chose San Francisco State for its hands-on Broadcast and Electronic Communication Arts (BECA) program. The program offered real-world experience in television, video, audio, radio, digital production, multimedia, scriptwriting, and media business. I was hooked from day one. My passion for broadcasting grew stronger, and I knew I was on the right path.

I also took part in internships that were pivotal in shaping my passion for journalism. During my time at KRON—an independent station now, but the NBC affiliate in the San Francisco Bay Area in 1999—I faced discouragement when someone suggested that my accent might not be suitable for English TV. This made me hesitant to pursue on-camera work. However, rather than letting this deter me, I became determined to enhance my skills. Just when I was about to give up on on-camera work, a newscast editor, who was about to launch a Latin-inspired show called *Latin Eyes*, invited me to join the cast as a reporter. I seized the opportunity because it not only embraced accents and my Latinidad but also allowed me to showcase the diversity of Hispanic Americans and our cultures. I gladly accepted, and thus, my on-camera career was born in 1999, reporting and educating the San Francisco Bay Area market about the rich diversity within Latino/Hispanic culture. The cast members came from various backgrounds across Latin America and the Caribbean, from Cuba to Argentina, Spain, and Mexico.

When I first saw and heard myself on camera, I became very

aware of my accent, making me self-conscious. This prompted me to take voice, acting, and singing lessons to improve my accent. Despite hesitating about concealing my bilingualism, I was determined to enhance my abilities. Three decades later, I realize that being bilingual is not a limitation but a valuable asset. And, yes, I still have my accent. It doesn't hurt that celebrities like Sofia Vergara and Salma Hayek make accents not just cool, but downright irresistible. Who wouldn't want to sound like they're delivering a punchline or a passionate speech, even when just ordering a coffee?

CHANGE IS GOOD

In 2013, I made the tough decision to retire from my broadcasting career just two years after welcoming my first child, Luke, into the world. As I assessed the high daycare costs and compared them to my income as an executive producer, I realized that the numbers didn't add up.

I found myself at a crossroads, wanting to pursue fulfilling professional opportunities and satisfying my passion while being a dedicated mother who is present for my child. This realization prompted me to seek new paths that would allow me to grow in my career without compromising my role as a parent. Ultimately, I wanted to find a balance that would help me thrive personally and professionally. When I left broadcasting after almost sixteen years, I felt like my world was crashing down. Broadcasting had been my identity; without it, I felt lost. However, during my short time as a stay-at-home mom, friends in public relations (PR) saw potential in me, suggesting I could excel in communications and PR. Their belief in me reignited my confidence.

Through my transition to PR, I wanted to continue to share stories that inform and inspire, as I did in news. I evolved from a journalist to a professional communicator, grateful for the connections made in the television world and also thankful that I had inside knowledge of what producers and reporters needed to cover a story.

My nearly twenty-year career in television news taught me invaluable PR skills, such as building relationships, problem-solving, research, and effective and strategic communication. While booking guests, producing newscasts, writing copy and managing investigative pieces, I honed my ability to think on my feet and adapt to fast-paced, high-pressure environments. These experiences seamlessly transitioned into my PR career, where the precision and creativity I developed became vital assets. I learned that every skill I acquired was a steppingstone to my future success, each contributing to a robust foundation in PR and marketing foundation. The rigorous demands of television news fostered a deep understanding of audience engagement, message crafting, and crisis management, which are crucial in PR.

As a Latina professional working in PR, my cultural background greatly influences how I approach my work. My unique superpower lies in an ability to offer a distinct perspective, drawing from my bilingual and bicultural identity. This allows me to craft messages that resonate with diverse audiences, incorporating cultural relevance into communications strategies.

Being a Latina in PR has its unique set of advantages and challenges. On the positive side, my cultural background provides me with a diverse perspective that enriches my approach to communication. I understand Latino audiences, which is invaluable in crafting authentic and relatable messages. Being bilingual allows me to bridge language gaps and connect with a broader audience. However, there are also cons, such as the occasional need to combat biases and misconceptions. One example is when people see me and say, "Oh, I may have a client for you that needs to translate a press release." To work with these challenges, I focus on showcasing my expertise as a communications professional, building strong professional relationships, and continuously educating myself and others about the value of diversity in PR and strategic communications.

Public relations holds significant importance as it plays a pivotal role in shaping public perception and influencing societal narratives. I feel a strong connection to this industry because it provides a platform to amplify the voices of underrepresented communities and promote inclusivity. PR professionals have the ability to forge genuine connections between brands and various communities, thus making it a domain where meaningful impact and positive change can be realized.

My Latin American background provides a valuable edge in the field of public relations. It empowers me to incorporate genuine cultural elements into my projects, enabling campaigns to resonate more deeply and effectively with Latino audiences. By celebrating my cultural heritage, I can establish meaningful connections with diverse communities, establish trust, and foster long-term loyalty. Being fluent in both English and Spanish has proven to be an invaluable asset throughout my professional journey. This proficiency has unlocked many opportunities, ranging from collaborating with global clients to engaging with Spanish-language media platforms. I encourage fellow bilingual individuals to embrace this skill, actively seeking roles prioritizing language diversity and leveraging it to bridge communication divides in multicultural environments.

In PR, like in TV news, I had to learn independently, constantly evolving and adapting. The statement "I'll figure it out" became my motto and built in me the desire to be more resourceful and to be the resource that others may need. I learned that being a lifelong learner is the best way to live. One of my first jobs after the TV world was at the California Governor's Office of Emergency Services (Cal OES) as a public information officer (PIO), where I served as a spokesperson and media strategist. One of the main reasons I took that job was that the department manager called our office "The Newsroom" and it made me feel like I was still working in a newsroom when I was coordinating interviews across the country and state, acting as an agency spokesperson and writing informational pieces for our website and blog. During my time at Cal OES, we launched an online show. I was excited to use the knowledge, skills, and abilities I had from my previous roles and complement the skills of my colleagues. I was still telling stories, producing videos, doing interviews, and managing high-pressure communication challenges during some of the many disasters we had to manage. I discovered that challenges are opportunities in disguise.

While supporting a significant disaster operation at the State Operations Center at Cal OES, I was recruited to work for the American Red Cross. I guess the CEO saw something in me—a rush to deliver information accurately or the positive adrenaline when asked to speak on camera or to support news reporters. I felt honored that someone would offer me a job while I was already employed!

During my tenure at the American Red Cross, I honed my PR skills and cultivated strong connections with media professionals. Following the birth of my second child, a seasoned industry expert encouraged me to transition into PR consulting. My initial clients were authors, and I leveraged my expertise to secure valuable press coverage for them. Each obstacle I encountered along the way only served to better prepare me for future success.

A NEW BEGINNING

In 2016, I took the leap and established my own consulting firm, SociosPR. It was then that I realized that there weren't many Latinas in Sacramento who were fully bilingual and bicultural, and after some research, I discovered that I was the only Latina-owned PR firm in the region. Today, the landscape has evolved, with many agencies listing multicultural communications as one of their core competencies. I am proud to know I've been paving the way for future generations in the industry.

Compared to US demographics, people of color are underrepresented in PR. Whites make up 76.5 percent of the population, while 83.6 percent of PR specialists. Latinos, Blacks, and Asians are also underrepresented.[1] The profession needs cultural competence, genuine respect for differences, and sensitivity to how culture affects perceptions. We must continue to break barriers and create opportunities for all.

Connecting with people from different backgrounds involves recognizing situational identity and handling PR with care based on thorough research. Diversity, multiculturalism, and inclusiveness play a vital role in PR, even though applying their meanings can be complex. Embracing these principles is key to building a more inclusive and empathetic global community.

Even when faced with doubts and stereotypes, I stayed focused and determined. For a long time, it frustrated me when individuals or agencies would reach out to me under the assumption that I was limited to just one skill, like Spanish translations, or that my work was confined to supporting nonprofits serving disenfranchised communities. Over time, I've learned to embrace those misconceptions as opportunities to demonstrate that my biculturalism is a unique strength. It allows me to excel in all facets of PR—from media relations and event planning to crisis communications and community engagement. My ability to navigate diverse projects and deliver results sets me apart as a dynamic and versatile communications professional.

---

[1] WPSU-Penn State Public Media, "Race and Ethnicity in the US and PR Workplace." https://archive.pagecentertraining.psu.edu/public-relations-ethics/introduction-to-diversity-and-public-relations/lesson-2-how-to-reach-diverse-stakeholders/key-concepts-and-approaches.

I envision a world where diversity is not only embraced, but also celebrated, where our differences and individual strengths are valued. I want to live in a world where everyone, regardless of their background, can seamlessly connect and communicate in the rich tapestry of today's diverse America.

Today, many brands are listening to diverse voices and using data to understand what really matters to people from all walks of life. When I read articles on what brands like Adobe, Target, and Pepsi are doing to show accurate representation of their customers, so they feel seen, heard, and understood, I get overjoyed and make every effort to learn from their strategies. I'm so glad that the world is becoming more accepting of differences. It's better than twenty years ago, so I call that progress. Their forward-thinking approach leads to stronger brands, happier customers, and greater success in diverse markets. I'm excited to be part of a movement that's putting people first.

The power of storytelling to create positive change and ignite inspiration in others has always fueled my passion.

VISIBILITY MOMENT

Throughout my career, I have consistently focused on promoting my clients' and teams' achievements and successes, ensuring their stories are told and celebrated. I've always adhered to the principle that there's no "I" in "team." However, it is crucial to reflect on our accomplishments, as they serve as milestones demonstrating our growth and the impact we've made. Reflecting on these moments teaches us to appreciate our journey, build confidence, and encourage others to embrace their achievements.

Doing so creates a ripple effect, inspiring those around us to step into the light and claim their successes.

I have a powerful tip to help you get started on your journey. A few years ago, during my morning quiet times, I began a transformative habit: I would write down three things I was grateful for and three things I was proud of each day. This practice of starting my day by acknowledging my accomplishments filled me with hope, pride, and confidence. I've continued this habit ever since, and its impact has been life-changing. Even simple acts, like consistently food journaling for a month or two, can create a positive ripple effect in our lives. Small steps can lead to monumental changes, and it's never too late to start.

BIOGRAPHY

Lilly Cortés Wyatt founded SociosPR, a leading integrated communications firm known for its commitment to cultural competence and inclusivity. With a career spanning over twenty-five years in media and public relations, Lilly has crafted strategies that resonate with diverse communities, drawing on her deep ties to the Greater Sacramento area. Her bilingual skills and intuitive understanding of multicultural communication have made her a respected leader in the field.

Starting as a broadcast journalist with major networks like NBC Universal, ABC, Univision, and Telemundo, Lilly's career has been marked by numerous accolades, including the prestigious Women Who Mean Business Award and various PRSA Influence Awards. Under her leadership, SociosPR has become a top PR agency in Sacramento and one of the fastest-growing companies in the region.

Born in Martinez, California, and raised in Mexico, Lilly embodies the vibrant bicultural identity of modern America. Outside of her professional achievements, Lilly enjoys being an active mom of two young boys (eight and twelve), a devoted home organizer, a wife, and a passionate believer and nature enthusiast who cherishes balancing her career with family life and outdoor adventures.

Lilly Cortés Wyatt
Instagram: @sociospr
LinkedIn: Lilly Cortés Wyatt

THE ART OF THE PIVOT

BRENDA DURAN

"What looked like a closed door and the end of one career turned into a new, unexpected, and fulfilling career."

THE BLUEPRINT IS YOU

The memory is etched in my brain like it was yesterday. I was in my eleventh-grade English class when, one day, my teacher, Mr. Thompson, pulled me aside to tell me he felt I needed to leave his class and be placed in the Advanced Placement (AP) English cohort taught by Mr. Halle. I had outgrown his regular English class, he said, and I belonged in the higher-level cohort. I remember being stunned. Me? The former English as a Second Language (ESL) kid headed to AP English? No way, I thought, that is way outside of my comfort zone.

Weeks later, I was sitting among the other AP students, and feelings of inadequacy and fear of the unknown crept up on me. The feelings were so strong that I rushed to Mr. Halle's office after week one and pleaded with him, with tears in my eyes, to drop me from the class because I felt I would not cut it. What happened next would change the entire trajectory of my life and career.

Mr. Halle firmly said no. He refused to drop me from the class and told me I had everything it took to succeed and belonged in the class just like the others. He ripped up my written request, tossed it in the trash, and asked me to start embracing my potential with open arms and be open to going to new places because I had what it takes. So, I did. I showed up the entire semester scared and confused, and with little confidence, I could pull it off. But I left with more self-assurance than I expected and the determination I would need decades later.

These are the same feelings I had when I decided to leave my career in journalism to embark on my new career as a newly minted public relations (PR) professional. Scared, unable to see the other side yet, deep inside, I knew I was armed with the skills and foundation I needed to succeed. I just had to take the leap.

STORIES TO TELL

Storytelling is part of my DNA. I have been fascinated with stories since childhood; the curious child in me has never left. I knew early on that I wanted to be a storyteller. I wrote my first book in the first grade in Ms. Candelaria's classroom.

I was given a chance to create a book with my own vision and even got to choose the colors for the cover—purple (my favorite) and pink. It was part autobiographical and part fiction, sprinkled with fragments of my wild imagination, like the page where I claimed to own dozens of kites and spent my summers visiting my grandmother in Mexico at a cantina.

When I was old enough to know this type of innate curiosity could become a career, I was intrigued. When I found out what journalism was, I latched on to it and wanted to be part of that club more than anything in the world. I wrote for the student newspaper in high school. I moved on to run the Talon Marks newspaper in community college. I set my sights on getting into the big leagues—the prestigious University of Southern California Annenberg School for Communication and Journalism in Los Angeles. I thought I needed that highly coveted journalism degree to take off and make it in the world. As a first-generation Mexican-American, I always dreamed of taking my parents' sacrifices to the next level.

Many of us can relate to this.

I am the youngest daughter of two Mexican immigrants who came to the United States nearly fifty years ago after chasing their own dreams of wanting to open infinite worlds of opportunity for their children. Like many other first-generation kids, my parents never learned to speak English as they were too focused on ensuring our basic needs were met by working long hours, leaving the day-to-day tasks to my older siblings.

We did not have conversations about grades, careers, or college in our house. Some may have seen this as a deterrent to success, but I saw it as a way to grow as an independent individual determined to figure it out and learned early on that I had to depend on my grit to get by. Much later, I realized that although my parents' influence on my career choices was not always front and center, the freedom they gave me to daydream was all I needed to craft my vision for what I wanted in my life and career. Their work ethic has always been imprinted in me, and their bold moves have inspired me to make a few of my own in more ways than one.

We have all gained from the sacrifices of our parents and have known they were the gateway to our own dreams. I always had a fascination with hearing the stories my parents talked about — their former lives in their home country and their journey to a new life in the United States.

My father could always recount his early years working as a bracero (US guest worker) with such precision that you can easily visualize what it must have been like for him to work the cotton fields and agriculture sites around the US while dreaming of a new life for him and his family. Growing up, I felt like a natural communicator who was destined to share stories like theirs and others in the future. Like many things I set out to do in my life, I did, and it came with many unexpected detours.

CHASING THE DREAM

First came the prestigious internships—*El Paso Times,*

PEOPLE magazine, and *The Denver Post.* Then came the jobs. For the first few years out of college, I was a devoted print journalist working in North County San Diego, covering Latino issues and education. I embedded myself in people's lives and retold their heartfelt stories of struggle, redemption, and success to live on forever in ink. My parents were proud. I was proud to be one of the few Latinas working in a newsroom—being the "voice to the voiceless." But that dream was short-lived, and I quickly learned that the illusion that a career was a straight and narrow path would never be a reality.

As the digital revolution took off and a recession loomed, my career journey of twists and turns began. I left my first newspaper job as talks of layoffs began to circulate and went back home to do entertainment news. However, newspapers were my first love, and I wasn't ready to break up yet. But, one day, it turned out, newspapers would break up with me as layoffs rolled out during hard times in the print industry.

The reality of the world began to set in. It was hard. When there is no blueprint, you seek paths, models, and a point of reference, even if there is none.

There were no sounding boards, mentors, or roadmap to refer to. It took me nearly a decade to see the experience for what it was—a life lesson in redirection and the armor I needed to grow in order to face life's curveballs along the way. This is the experience many of you will face in your careers, just like our parents, who had no blueprint themselves. We have to be the trailblazers and set the path forward first.

We are bred for this. Our ancestors faced unimaginable obstacles and adversity. We are capable of what they were capable of and much more. Courage runs in our bloodline.

EMBRACING THE UNKNOWN

In Fall 2019, heartbroken, I made the bold move to leave print journalism behind. It was not a decision I made with resolve but instead with grief and confusion about what to do next. I had yet to learn the meaning of the term "transferable skills" and had not really ventured out of the industry I studied and focused so heavily on for years. But the rollercoaster of emotions and lack of reciprocity from journalism led me to take a blind leap of faith forward. It required me to shed an identity I had worked so hard for and embrace fear of the unknown. How would I do that? All I had to do was think back to Mr. Halle's wise words: "You have what it takes."

Venturing into a new career is hard. It involves learning a new language, learning a new way of life, and acknowledging that the original vision you set out for yourself did not come to fruition. When I decided to use my storytelling skills in PR, it felt like I was jumping off a cliff blindfolded.

But we have learned to do this our whole lives as Latinas. We have learned to succeed without a safety net time and time again.

I applied to work in government PR for Los Angeles County on a whim with little expectation. I did not fully grasp what the job would entail, but somehow, I knew it would take me places I had not yet experienced as a well-rounded storyteller and communicator.

I quickly learned that being a PR professional requires being a great storyteller. This is an essential skill for succeeding in the profession. Along the way, I began to see how my journalism skills seamlessly aligned with my new job running government communication initiatives and campaigns.

A decade later, I am on the other side now, with a keen sense of what makes a good story and a seamless PR operation, as well as what people want to hear and how to best achieve it. I still marvel at how my journalism foundation allowed me to excel in my new PR career path.

As a journalist, I ran my own magazine for one of the largest cities in California, managing multiple staff and a large budget, art-directing photo shoots, and planning the editorial line-up. As a PR professional, I have been tasked with running $1 million marketing campaigns for the largest county in the country and building out functional communication teams from scratch.

In the past decade, I have become a storyteller who can easily translate complex issues into stories that resonate, and have expanded my skill set as a storyteller by creating public service announcements like I did as a journalist through articles.

Like journalism, working as a government PR professional has allowed me to tell the stories that matter in our lives and be of public service. I could not have found the success I have without my journalism foundation.

And just like that, it all came full circle.

What looked like a closed door and the end of one career turned into a new, unexpected, and fulfilling career. Leaving the fear behind and seeing a new vision for myself was a recurring lesson I had to embrace yet again.

I love Steve Jobs' quote, "You cannot connect the dots moving forward, only looking back." That is exactly what I have experienced, pivoting from being a journalist to a PR professional.

Being a PR professional can be challenging and rewarding, just like being a journalist. Public relations has allowed me to blend creativity, strategy, and relationship-building into a new career path that keeps the work interesting and impactful.

To get to this realization a decade later, I had to let go of fear and expectations. I had to return to the feelings I had in Mr. Halle's classroom and fully embrace my potential because I was ready for something new, even if I could not see it. I had to go back to embracing the daring spirit of my immigrant parents and make new leaps for a better future. I had to take all my experiences and know they would serve as stepping stones for the next big move. Only when I opened myself to embracing the pivot could I expand my career and future and succeed as a Latina PR professional.

I want you to know that, at times, the path will seem blurry, confusing, and, yes, even daunting. Often, the answers will not be there for you, and you may find yourself lost. You will encounter the hard task of reinventing yourself more than once, and I am here to let you know that, in the end, it will all be worth it.

Without those experiences, you would not have the compelling stories to tell future generations. Without those experiences, you won't be able to fulfill your full potential—even the one you do not see in front of you yet. Without the detours, you will not be able to create what we all have inside of us—the ability to create a blueprint for others to succeed.

Keep going. You will marvel at what is waiting on the other side if you can get out of your own way, just like I was reminded of that one day in that AP English classroom.

You are the blueprint.

VISIBILITY MOMENT

As a first-generation Latina, promoting myself has been crucial to my career journey. Early in my career, I worked in an industry where I made up 1 percent of Latinas working in print newspapers. My contributions were often overlooked. I realized that to advance and make a meaningful impact, I had to be my own advocate. I learned that it was my duty to highlight my achievements in meetings, volunteer for high-visibility projects, and share my successes with my network. Others need to see you. We cannot be what we cannot see. Making myself visible was my mission and a responsibility I felt toward those coming up behind me. This proactive approach not only showcased my value to the organizations I have worked for but has also opened doors to leadership opportunities and professional growth that I might have otherwise missed.

Reflecting on one's accomplishments as a first-generation Latina is especially important because it highlights the unique challenges and barriers we've overcome. This reflection allows us to see how our perseverance and hard work have paved the way not only for our success but also for future generations. It teaches us the value of our cultural heritage and the strength derived from our community and family support. Acknowledging our achievements builds a stronger sense of identity and pride, which fuels our confidence and resilience. This practice also serves as a reminder of the importance of paving the way for others, reinforcing our role as trailblazers and advocates within our communities.

BIOGRAPHY

Brenda Duran is a highly accomplished media and communications specialist with a notable decade-long tenure in Los Angeles County. Significant contributions in key roles have marked her career, including Communications Director for the Los Angeles County Registrar-Recorder County Clerk and Deputy Executive Officer of Communications and Creative Services at the Executive Office of the Los Angeles County Board of Supervisors, and Director of External Affairs for the newly established Los Angeles County Justice, Care, and Opportunities Department. In these positions, she played a pivotal role in initiating and expanding the social media presence of the departments, significantly enhancing their public outreach and overseeing the development of their communications office infrastructure from the ground up.

Brenda's expertise lies in crafting strategic and concise messaging for a wide array of public programs and initiatives. Her portfolio includes the successful launch of numerous multimedia campaigns spanning various mediums, such as editorial, TV, radio spots, social media engagement, outdoor billboards, and public service announcements endorsed by notable public figures. She also has excelled in developing comprehensive communication plans and directing social media strategy in times of crisis.

Prior to her illustrious career in Los Angeles County, Brenda made her mark in print media as a newspaper reporter and magazine editor. In this capacity, she oversaw the implementation of various digital platforms to expand the reach of content online and in print.

Brenda's educational background is rooted in journalism, having earned a bachelor of arts degree from the University of Southern California Annenberg School for Communication and Journalism in Los Angeles. Her diverse experiences and extensive skill set place her at the forefront of media and communications, making her a vital contributor to the success of various public programs and initiatives in Los Angeles County.

She is the youngest daughter of Segundo and Rosa Duran, two Mexican immigrants who set out for the American dream nearly fifty years ago.

Brenda Duran
LinkedIn: Brenda Duran
Website: www.bduran.com

THE ROAD TO MY PUBLIC RELATIONS CAREER

AMELIA TAUREL FOLKES, MPS, APR

"The support of Latinas in my life and the network of allies I've built along the way made my journey enlightening and exciting."

MY JOURNEY

I like to describe my journey into public relations (PR) as a winding road—filled with yield signs, multiple lanes, and a few speed bumps. But what has truly guided me throughout my career are the fantastic women who have acted as my guides—*mis guías*—directing me along the way or sometimes driving me to get in the right lane. I may have thought I knew where I was going, but I wasn't always in the driver's seat of my destiny. The support of many Latinas in my life and the network of allies I've built along the way made my journey enlightening and exciting.

To begin with, I had never heard of the PR profession until college and didn't see myself in this profession. I thought my path was to solve world peace through global affairs and public policy work. I was going to join the Peace Corps and then the United Nations. I studied Latin American policy because of all the injustice that had taken place in Central and South America.

As a Latina born to immigrant parents from Colombia and Argentina, I knew firsthand about the injustice and struggle of immigrant families. Our family's experiences in Houston, including receiving bomb threats at our home and facing discrimination, were a stark reminder of the downsides of being an immigrant family in Texas in the 1980s. These experiences, while instilling fear, also fueled my determination to fight for justice and embrace my cultural identity.

Throughout my life, I was fortunate to be surrounded by powerful women, including my mother, who supported me and urged me to go to college. I would be the first in my family to do so. I thought I knew what my destiny would be once I was there, studying public policy. However, something changed after I took a crisis communications class to fulfill coursework as part of my journalism minor. I was not even excited about taking this class. However, during a group assignment, we had to get up in front of the class and hold a mock press conference after a client crisis. My professor grilled our team, and I was on fire with answers to protect our client's reputation. I think my defenses kicked in from childhood experiences. Afterward, my professor applauded our work and asked if I had considered pursuing PR. I hadn't, but that day, a new career path opened up, sparking a newfound excitement and inspiration.

THE SPARK IGNITED

A few years later, now married and living in California, I worked for San Diego Dialogue, a nonprofit public policy center researching cross-border issues. It was an ideal job because I could use my Spanish skills with officials in Tijuana and utilize my degree. Unfortunately, I quickly learned that I didn't love the world of public policy research as much as I thought I would. The challenges were significant, especially being surrounded by an all-white academic male environment in the 1990s and often being asked as a young Latina, "to make the coffee, sweetheart" was quite a turn-off. The funny thing was I didn't even know how to make coffee.

I started to think I had wasted my time pursuing my degree. However, this organization allowed me to stretch my skills and try different things, like event planning, newsletter production, and media outreach. We worked for a visionary leader who wanted to do great things for the San Diego/Tijuana region, so he brought in high-profile dignitaries for policy talks.

The first big event was with the then-Attorney General Janet Reno. This was my next spark. I learned so much from a wonderful Latina team member about managing difficult situations gracefully, even when the men in the room didn't respect me. She encouraged me to do more, look forward, and use my bilingual skills as an opportunity to grow. I was young, barely out of college, and unaware that something had changed for me. *My path had veered into a new lane.*

I also didn't realize at this time that the public relations/communications profession included so many different skill sets, such as event planning, production, messaging, script writing, editing, and coordinating with VIPs as part of the job. I was so lucky to have learned this early on in my career.

After this job, I began to look for other roles in the communications field. I took any role because I wanted to learn more since I hadn't studied it in college. I worked for another nonprofit, helping write grants to support the technology sector, and then a bath manufacturer as a part-time translator and PR assistant. I got to flex my Spanish and media relations skills on toilets and sinks! These unexpected opportunities in the PR industry taught me to be open to new possibilities and to embrace them with enthusiasm. I also get to tell lots of funny stories about translating sales and PR stuff about toilets. It turns out that being bilingual became an advantage when I was looking for PR jobs as I moved around the country.

My next significant opportunity in PR was when I joined FleishmanHillard (FH) after moving to Austin, Texas. I learned so much about the industry and my profession here. Being bilingual and having a policy background also allowed me to work on a groundbreaking account for the newly created US Department of Homeland Security on southern border issues—a truly rewarding opportunity to flex my skills and deepen relationships with other Latinas.

My boss was a great mentor and instilled in me the importance of being a leader who cares about her team and brings those up around you. Her guidance and the opportunities she provided were instrumental in my career growth. My time at FH was truly transformative, and I always recommend working for a PR agency to students when looking for internships or their first job in the industry.

While at FH, I was fortunate to be introduced to *Las Comadres Para Las Americas,* a group of Latinas who had a profound impact on my life. The Latinas I met through this organization were pivotal in my personal and professional growth. Here, I truly learned that connections are the key to a successful road ahead.

UNEXPECTED TURNS IN MY CAREER

After a few years and two kids, I took an in-house communications role with State Farm. My career took off during my time here, and I got to stretch my communication muscles and use my bilingual skills again. Working in-house is very different from working at a PR firm. The intensity and speed can sometimes be slower, and you become an expert in one area since you are now working for just one client. This made me think my career path would be straight and with fewer turns. As it turns out, it was bumpy and had several left and right turns.

I had found my groove and worked with a great team and manager. A fellow Latina! I explored many different areas of PR, from crisis communications (that class finally paid off) to community affairs and disaster response. I was even the team lead for multicultural PR and counseled the rest of our team on Spanish media outreach.

One day, my manager told me it was time to spread my wings and try something new, and she took me off her team to join the brand team and forced me to change lanes. At first, I thought I had done something wrong and felt unwanted, but I learned this manager saw something in me that I didn't even see in myself. I have no idea how she knew to push me, but my career took off in ways I would never have imagined. I got to work on some amazing national campaigns with celebrities and major media outlets, helping mentor peers and work on award-winning campaigns. It was scary to jump from the slow lane to the fast lane, but fun.

Another significant aspect of my time at State Farm was when I staffed a conference for the National Council of La Raza (NCLR), now known as UnidosUS. I was at a cocktail event when a fellow Latina looked at me and said, "Why don't you have a master's degree?" I was stunned and had a zillion excuses, but what she said after that stuck with me. "We need more Latinas with graduate degrees to show them we can." She didn't say who the "them" was, but I think I knew who they were. It could be our families, our daughters, the white men telling me to get them coffee. I believe it was one or two years later that I enrolled in a graduate program. I don't know her name, but here on these pages, I say "thank you" for giving me that shove I needed. I never envisioned myself in graduate school, but I did it. First in my family to do so.

The great thing about working for a large corporation is that I could go back to school, earn my accreditation in PR, attend many professional development conferences, and mentor PRSSA students, all with the support of my team. I wouldn't have done any of those things if I hadn't been pushed to do so by Latinas along the way.

LOOKING IN MY REARVIEW MIRROR

While I was grateful for the opportunities at State Farm, I wanted to explore new adventures. I swerved into a new lane and tried my hand at thought leadership, environmental sustainability and cybersecurity communications for global technology companies. The work was fast paced and thrilling, but something was missing for me, which brings me to my current role. I headed back to my roots and now work at Raise Your Hand Texas, a non-partisan policy nonprofit that advocates for public education in Texas. I am excited to leverage all my skills in media relations, thought leadership, content development, and brand reputation in this role. I am utilizing my bilingual skills and have helped the organization broadly and effectively reach the Hispanic community for the first time with important topics in public education. I have been able to connect my policy background, passion for reaching underrepresented communities, and expertise in communications in this current role. It is one of the most rewarding of my career, especially because I get to work for another talented leader who fosters my professional growth.

As I look back on my career's rearview mirror, I have had

many great bosses and teammates, but some of the best have been fellow women who have given of themselves by teaching me, pushing me, and showing me how to lead with grace.

HAVE AN ADVISORY COUNCIL

An informal advisory council keeps me from being so scared that I don't try things. Everyone will say to have a mentor and find your allies, which are indeed important. But I say, create your advisory council, too. It can include peers in the industry you don't work with directly but understand the business. They can be friends or colleagues you meet at conferences. This is what *Las Comadres* was for me for many years. I now have new "councils" of talented women I connect with and who help each other grow.

I learned that feeling alone or scared to try something new are normal feelings, but using your connections and leaning on those guiding you along your journey—*tus guías*—makes it all worth it. This is still hard for me, so I take it one day or one turn on my road at a time.

Throughout my career, I have been fortunate to have the guidance and support of incredible Latinas who have shaped my path and inspired me to strive for excellence. Their mentorship has helped me achieve my professional goals and fueled my passion for creating a more equitable and inclusive workplace.

I want to thank one specific Latina, Audrey Ponzio, the founding partner of APC Collective, for sponsoring my story in this book. I am sharing today because of her support. I want to express my heartfelt gratitude. *¡Gracias, amiga!*

VISIBILITY MOMENT

As a Latina in PR, I've witnessed firsthand how cultural biases and stereotypes can hinder professional advancement. This has reinforced my commitment to mentor students of diverse backgrounds and advocate for inclusivity in our industry. My years of experience as a Latina in the PR field have profoundly shaped my understanding of the systemic barriers, highlighting the urgent need for more diversity in our profession, especially for those of the Black, Indigenous, and people of color (BIPOC) community. For this reason, I am unapologetic about who I am and my background. I never hide or underestimate the power of my bilingual skills with potential clients or future employers because it has opened doors to a broader range of opportunities for me, and ensured our community is represented in the work I have done.

No path is ever direct or straight; sometimes, you should go for it when someone pushes you into a new lane. Lean on those around you because they can help you, even those personal relationships. I always say the field of public relations is small and connected—meaning you keep contacts, no matter how long it's been or where you live. The number of times an opportunity has presented itself because of a relationship I made in the past is numerous. I encourage others to embrace their cultural identity as a strength and seek out mentors who can provide guidance and support. Build a strong network of allies, colleagues, peers, and supporters, within and outside of the PR industry. These connections can be invaluable as you navigate your career.

The most important part is to reflect on your journey along the way. Pause and see if you are heading in the right direction. And if not, it is okay to take a turn. As you read in my story, I did many times. I accomplished a lot and have more to do, but I also took many different roads to get there.

BIOGRAPHY

Amelia Taurel Folkes, MPS, APR is an award-winning communications professional based in Austin, Texas. She is the director of public relations for Raise Your Hand Texas where she oversees communication campaigns that support the organizations statewide regional advocacy team and the mission to advance the reputation of strategic priorities across policy, advocacy, and legislative engagement.

Prior to joining Raise Your Hand, she worked for large multinational firms supporting the C-suite with thought leadership communications, focusing on cybersecurity, ESG (environmental, social, and governance), and brand reputation issues. She also worked at State Farm for 11 years in community relations, catastrophe response and brand strategy. She managed Texas-based grant programs that positively impacted students, schools, and education-based nonprofits across Texas.

Folkes worked with clients such as the Department of Homeland Security, Hispanic Scholarship Fund, Office of National Drug Control Policy, AT&T, and others at the internationally recognized PR firm FleishmanHillard. Her work has won several awards, including a Public Relations Society of America (PRSA) Silver Anvil, PRSA Award of Excellence, and a PR Daily Non-Profit Communications finalist award.

Folkes is fluent in Spanish and has extensive experience researching issues dealing with access to education for underserved communities and working with multicultural audiences. Throughout her professional career, she has supported diversity initiatives, including starting or leading employee resource groups, mentoring Latinas, supporting research on Latinas in PR, and more. She has also helped mentor many PR students in their careers.

She holds a bachelor of arts in Latin American Studies from Texas A&M University and a master of professional studies in Strategic Public Relations from George Washington University. She received her professional Accreditation in Public Relations in 2016 and continues to stay active in PRSA.

Amelia Taurel Folkes, MPS, APR
LinkedIn: Amelia Folkes

THE POWER OF FALLING FORWARD

JEANNETTE E. GARCIA

"Our greatest failures can lead us to better opportunities in the long run, and my career is a testament to that theory."

It's okay to cry. Public relations is a hard field.

I am a Mexican-American woman from the Far Eastside of San Antonio. I have anxiety and admit that lately, I have been waking up at 3 a.m. with random spurts of inspiration and ideas that take away my slumber. These ideas are spurred by my professional experiences and inspired by random messages from people I have worked with, whether in a 9-to-5 job or one of the many volunteer jobs I have had in my career.

While I have met amazing professionals in the 9-to-5s,

those volunteer jobs have been some of the largest catalysts that have propelled my public relations (PR) and journalism career.

The chance encounters, such as serving on a board like that of the San Antonio Association of Hispanic Journalists or having a coffee or glass of wine, have led me to lead communications for my local municipality's economic development office, the local Hispanic Chamber of Commerce, and even convinced me to take a leap and become a journalist—the latter is a story that in itself could be a whole chapter.

But before we delve into my professional life, let me return to my personal background, which has also intrinsically shaped the person I have become.

I was raised by two loving parents who did the best they could with the means they had, which meant that at times, "the best" they could do was buy 99-cent Burger King Whopper sandwiches or 49-cent crunchy tacos and bean burritos from Taco Bell on Sundays. I grew up in what would be considered below the federal poverty level. However, with the love in my family household, I never thought much about the missing financial means.

Some moments and glimpses during high school made me realize I was living a life below means. At a recent event hosted by one of our local news outlets, I got to sit with a former administrator of my high school and remember telling him it wasn't until my time at the University of Texas at Austin (UT Austin) that I realized that my high school life was abnormal and that I felt like the token Latina girl added into the Gifted and

Talented program, which only had a handful of persons of color in it.

At UT Austin, surrounded by people who took for granted the Mercedes-Benzes and BMWs that their parents had given them, I realized I was actually poor. With the love of my *familia*, I felt I had it all.

IT'S OKAY TO FAIL AND TAKE A STEP BACK

In college, I networked extensively and was on the executive boards of many student-led organizations, including my sorority, Lambda Theta Alpha Latin Sorority, Inc., our Greek Council, and other multicultural organizations.

I held multiple internships, and after I received my bachelor's degree, I landed my first job at a small marketing agency recommended by one of my sorority sisters who also worked there. This led to one of my most humbling career experiences.

The PR department at this agency was in flux. There was turmoil with the current director of that department, and without a stable director, I learned from a fellow peer how to cold call journalists and pitch our client's story. The target audience for this client—a subsidized mobile phone plan—was mainly in small rural towns with the smallest print publications. We were already working off of a pre-made media list. At the time, I thought I was learning best practices, but now looking back, I see that many PR principles were lacking.

While I thought I was growing as a professional and quickly excelling at that job because I received three promotions in two years—going from a measly paid consultant role and ending my tenure as a full-time public relations account executive who managed a client's Medicare Advantage communication efforts. I was not growing the foundational skills that are needed from a good PR pro.

At the tender age of twenty-three, I also had no idea how to properly manage a program aimed at a demographic nearly three times my age. Despite the promotions and an overinflated ego, I was too inexperienced to actually handle that account.

It was overwhelming trying to lead an account at the time. I made my first media tour visits alone with the client, did not know how to report back on analytics properly, and did not have a leader who actually mentored and flourished young talent. I failed miserably and got fired for it.

The feeling of getting fired after so many quick promotions within my first two professional years after college humbled me. I felt lost. And yes, I cried. And I want to remind you it's okay to cry.

But my upbringing with hard-working parents and the networking lessons in college wouldn't let me stay down.

In typical fashion, I had already started getting involved in the previously mentioned professional organizations. While I felt defeated without a job, I continued on the grind through hard work in volunteer positions.

The forced respite from work also drew me to the realization that perhaps, just as Icarus flew too close to the sun, I needed to take a step back and go to a job that would help me further hone the foundational PR skills of pitching to media, collecting analytics, and building truly mutually beneficial relationships with the media so that I wouldn't completely flounder in this profession. I also knew I wanted to avoid the extreme chaos of agency life.

Whatever my next job would be, it would be in internal communications, even if it meant taking a pay cut. I knew my next move would require me to lower my ego and take a step back, which is the complete opposite of what all professional coaches would advise in a traditional career trajectory. But sometimes, taking a step back is exactly what you need to reset yourself. And it takes a major blow to your ego to come to that realization.

My next job required a nearly $10,000 pay cut, but more than a decade later, as I reflect on this move, I know it was the right step for me in my career.

At my next job, I worked in the corporate communications team for a research and consultancy firm. My internal clients and the global team of PR professionals were all brilliant minds.

I learned lessons from my peers in Argentina, Italy, and India, as well as from a director who knew how to provide constructive and growth-minded feedback. I learned how to properly write unique pitch topics to journalists, track metrics and update media lists, and develop media partnerships with trade publications.

I also honed my editing skills by ensuring that articles

written and sought out by our thought-leader consultants and research analysts, many of whom spoke English as a second language, were in a spot our media partners could easily place in their publications, including a Forbes contributor blog.

These were the basics I lacked in real-world experience before and needed to grow to truly have the basics to thrive in the PR field. I felt prepared and back on track to move up in my career. A blaze of fire in me extended into my next career few jumps.

QUITTING IS SOMETIMES THE BEST CHOICE

Let's fast-forward to the middle of my career; I felt a moment of professional existential dread. By this time in my career, I had led communications for royal visits to San Antonio and large economic development projects. I served on planning committees for some of our region's largest galas. I had successfully pitched stories for research analysts and consultants to outlets like the *Los Angeles Times, CNN,* and the *Detroit Free Press* and even landed a front-page mention in *The New York Times.* I was my local chapter's Public Relations Society of America's Horizon Award winner, which is given to rising stars in our profession.

Yet, I was entering the middle of my career in a situation where I felt like I was giving it my all and using every single PR tactic that had helped me to succeed thus far. However, I could not satisfy or meet the expectations of a new boss.

The constant non-constructive criticism of my work made

my cortisol levels rise to an unhealthy level. This person would verbally approve deliverables and state it was fine to send them to staff as final versions via email, only for them to "reply-all" and state that they wanted additional edits. I would cry almost every day after work. The feeling of making mistakes, even though I hadn't made them, was defeating.

Prior to this new boss, the work environment was fast-paced but tolerable, and work/life boundaries were allowed. The toxicity of the work environment under this new leader made me feel like a failure again, leading to a confidence nosedive that led to me actually making mistakes. I would go to work and hated my choice of career. I didn't want to do it anymore.

I thought of what it would be like to potentially go to a coding school or get another trade under my belt that wasn't in such a stressful environment. I am not a quitter, but I had to make a tough choice. For my own sanity, I decided to resign from this position.

After the resignation, I felt a weight lift off my shoulders. It was nearly half a year of mental torture I withstood from that person. The mental anguish it caused, though, was lasting and did make me question my worth as a communications professional.

Studies have shown that the long-term effects of stress can adversely affect our brains, particularly our memory and judgment. The long-term stress also made me wonder if I was any good at my profession.

As I established earlier, I am also not from a family with generational wealth. So, I needed to find a new job.

As a storyteller at heart and with a community-wide reputation of being a hard worker, I was able to land another job fairly quickly, but in the adjacent field of journalism. The pay scale was lateral, but the ability to further hone my nose for newsworthiness and my writing armed me with an elevated skill set and a new-found street cred and reputation among journalists who see me as a former peer.

While I did have to submit a fair share of daily articles, the work felt more manageable. The rush of breaking stories also provided a similar feeling of landing the story and my confidence rose again. I also had editors who were very open to hearing me out and challenged my growth, while also helping steer me toward the root of stories when I had writer's block. Ultimately, though, I missed the world of PR and returned to a job that provided me with ample days off and a competitive salary.

MY VISIBILITY MOMENT

Getting fired or having to quit are never pleasant situations. As a Latina, the resiliency I gained from my upbringing and the ability to bootstrap and make things work with limited means have helped me bounce back from both of these situations. While I would not want to experience these two scenarios again, they helped shape me professionally. Ultimately, I landed back on my feet in better work situations through hard work. I hope these experiences have also shown you, as a reader, that it is okay to fail. Our greatest failures can lead us to better opportunities in the long run, and my career is a testament to that theory. If you shed a few tears along the way, it doesn't make you weak. Remember, it's okay to cry every once in a while; it shows that you're human and that you care about your work.

As you go through your PR career, you have to build foundational skills such as writing, building authentic relationships with journalists, and continuously sharpen your networking skills so that people trust you and your work ethic. As a PR professional, your reputation and how people perceive you are essential to ensuring that if you fail miserably and find yourself in a situation without a job, you can bounce back limitedly unscathed.

BIOGRAPHY

Jeannette E. Garcia firmly believes that every moment of your life is an opportunity to learn and grow. As a first-generation college graduate and active community member, she also has first-hand experience knowing that education and programs that provide opportunities for students to co-mingle with people in positions of power are key to creating a more equitable future.

Jeanette is the Director of Communications at UP Partnership, a San Antonio systems-change organization. In the past, Jeannette was a reporter with the *San Antonio Business Journal* covering tech, defense, small business, and diversity, equity, and inclusion issues. She has more than a decade of communications, public relations, and marketing experience, having led these types of efforts for places like the San Antonio Hispanic Chamber of Commerce and the City of San Antonio's Economic Development Department. She has a bachelor's degree in public relations with concentrations in Latino Media Studies and Business Foundations from the University of Texas at Austin.

Jeannette E. Garcia
LinkedIn: Jeannette Garcia

A PUERTO RICAN WOMAN'S JOURNEY AND LEGACY IN PR

OLGA MAYORAL WILSON, MA, APR, FELLOW PRSA

"Like a ceiba standing tall, balancing in its strong roots and branches aiming at the skies, I taught myself to meet challenges by rebuilding every day."

Patience, perseverance, and persistence define my success in public relations (PR). These pillars have a transformative purpose . . . a power that I want to share with you.

I'm a Puerto Rican woman, an awards recipient in the PR industry, a PRSA Fellow, and an accredited member. I excel in everything I set my mind and heart to, be it as an educator, as diversity, equity and inclusion (DEI) advocate, as a two-time master's program alumni, or as a 2018 Texas State University President's Diversity Award recipient. Teaching research methods, writing, and PR campaigns to hundreds of young students was a rewarding experience because of its impact on young minds and because of the hope they represent.

Today, I'm retired but continue to be actively engaged in building the future as I did earlier. I have a passion for PR and offer my services through national committee work, improving and strengthening the organization's strategy-planning, national DEI committee, and PR Exam Accreditation Board research team. During the COVID-19 pandemic, I ran full speed ahead, regardless of pressures, disappointments, and inconveniences. Overall, it was an unusual learning experience.

Never a dull moment, I advocate through community/ nonprofit organizations making a difference, for example, with the San Antonio Area Foundation, Puerto Rican Heritage Society, churches, and schools. Of immense personal satisfaction and pride, I coordinated the 1947 oil painting donation by Puerto Rican artist Maria Luisa Penne-Rullan, my aunt, to the prestigious Ponce Museum of Art. And, I keep mentoring young professionals and university or Public Relations Student Society of America (PRSSA) students to prepare them to their PR careers.

These are my most recent sixteen years of a forty-five-year career journey, each based on patience, perseverance, and persistence seasoned with passion, faith, gratitude, and personal growth.

ESTABLISHING MY HISPANIC IDENTITY

Earlier, I focused on crisis communications management for Fortune 500 financial institutions. Every step is a lesson. Each one is both a challenge and an opportunity. Be always aware, observe with intention, and grab opportunities as they come. Just as I did, you'll find inner peace, depth, and perspective because inspiration and strength surround all of us.

We all have key influencers in our professional growth. Edward Bernays, considered the "father of public relations," was key. During a visit to San Juan, Bernays approached me upon seeing my maiden last name on my tag—Mayoral. Asking if I used it, I asserted. He shared that his wife started using her maiden name decades earlier, starting an unusual trend. Bernays considered it a sign of maturity, self-identity, and solid values. He encouraged me to use it always! Delighted at his words, I was inspired.

UNKNOWN CHALLENGES

In 1985, my husband was reassigned to Hawaii to fulfill his duties in the US Coast Guard (USCG), so we packed our bags and moved from San Juan to Hawaii. I believe that my challenges are synonymous with the strengths acquired. It's up to oneself to make it work! As a USCG military spouse novice transferring to Hawaii, I experienced unique "adventures." Three months away at sea and one month in port was my husband's new norm. It was stressful at times with no cellphones, minimal overseas phone calls, few friends, no regular mail, and job hunting. However, island-living was magical; each day brought surprises and unique and beautiful experiences. The rich Asia-Pacific-Hawaiian culture gifted us both with gratitude and treasures.

My optimistic attitude was present by nature. When I went from Puerto Rico to Hawaii, I was a senior executive working with big accounts so I felt very confident with my portfolio. I felt very secure that I would find a job very quickly as it showed unique Fortune 500 companies' successful PR cases (American Airlines, Walgreens, Colgate Palmolive and others). But, unbeknownst to me, I had entered a rabbit's hole—the "challenging world of a military spouse trying to gain employment."[2] I applied for jobs, but my queries went nowhere. What was happening? I kept steadily moving ahead with calls, introductions, and referrals. To keep myself busy while job hunting, I began volunteering to engage with my local community. Community involvement was and continues to be a key to my success! I recommend it as part of anyone's individual toolbox.

I met with the USCG ombudswoman, who introduced me to the Hawaii State Status Commission on Women PR chair. She became an excellent peer who recognized my career track. Proactive and understanding, she recruited me to serve as a PR volunteer. I learned to never let an opportunity go by. Though not a paying job, it opened many doors.

Afterward, I met other professionals and community leaders while adding local experience. I learned about the state's rich and diverse history. One time while interviewing, my interviewer suddenly ended our conversation when she found out I was

---

[2] MOAA. The Military Officers Association of America. Accessed July 1, 2024. https://www.moaa.org.

Puerto Rican. At first, I didn't understand, but it soon became apparent that I was being discriminated against. Although this was difficult, it changed my experience and I began to learn about and advocate for DEI and underserved communities.

Words of wisdom arrive in unexpected ways. I touched base with an acquaintance. He was welcoming, respectful, and considerate. He shared Hawaii's "lay of the land" and a powerful message, which I still follow today—nurture perseverance, patience, and persistence. His words, full of wisdom and kindness, gave me hope and inspiration when I most needed it.

A third interview led me to an interesting proposition for developing PR proposals, but it came with a catch. This catch was that the hours spent researching, analyzing, developing, and presenting those proposals would not be paid unless the client was secured. I was disappointed but persistent and optimistic, so I took the chance. To their surprise, in less than a month, I secured the first client—Hawaii State Seat Belt Law Coalition, a group comprised of government, private enterprises, and community groups engaged in promoting the use of seat belts. The USDOT and the US Auto Manufacturers Association in Detroit, Michigan, promoted it. Backed by our PR campaign, Hawaii's seat belt usage rate has led nationally. And I was paid throughout my involvement!

I learned that I lead the way with my cultural knowledge. Diversity, equity, and inclusion was not known. As a Puerto Rican woman, I led the forefront strategy building with DEI. Coordination with Hawaii's multicultural communities and multiple languages delivered the expected results. Known as grassroots efforts, the educational materials on seat belt law were translated into seven languages. The successful campaign received numerous accolades, the top being the reduction of highway deaths.

Others recognized my work ethic, values, and professional acumen. I caught their attention and was recruited first by the Hawaii State DOT-PR Division and later by its Airport Division. Our primary responsibilities were the Pacific Basin Initiative and communication of the airport infrastructure expansion and improvement in all of Hawaii's Islands. Its objectives were to improve the state's economy by promoting growth, modernizing airport infrastructure, increasing Hawaii's visitors' numbers, and accelerating visitors' entrance through US Immigration.

Professionally, I believe patience, perseverance, and persistence finally coincided like stars aligned in the sky to guide me. This opportunity opened doors and opportunities to learn about Pacific Rim countries' initiatives and taught me its state-federal legislative and geopolitical agenda strategies. It spearheaded my career from Hawaii to my next professional adventure in Washington, DC. Arriving in the nation's capital with a guaranteed contract as a public affairs lobbyist, I felt a deep sense of recognition and accomplishment in my new role serving Hawaii and, coincidentally, Puerto Rico.

My assignment was to represent Hawaii in DC's legislative and congressional committee sessions, communicate and monitor legislative initiatives aimed at improving the airport infrastructure, promote international air routes from Japan and Germany through the USDOT legal procedures, and identify and advocate for federal funding to build a new airport tower in San Juan's International Airport. Add the uniqueness of my roles at the Organization of American States (non-governmental office) and National Puerto Rican Coalition managing a USDOH CRA and Fair Housing/Fair Lending educational grant (English and Spanish) encompassing both Hispanics in Puerto Rico and mainland US.

Then, it was time to relocate once again, from DC back to Puerto Rico in 1997.

MY C-SUITE JOURNEY: SITTING AT THE TABLE

My visibility period started when I accepted the managing director position at Plus PR in San Juan. I maintained contact with its reporting partners—returning as their managing director from 1997 to 2002 was a sign of respect and validation. I reconnected and secured long-standing solid clients, such as Walgreens Co.

In 2002, Banco Popular identified me as a top candidate to manage their corporate PR division as senior vice president and manager. I led its five units, supervised thirty-plus employees, and managed its $12 million annual budget. I managed corporate communications, media relations, internal and community relations, BPPR Foundation, and visual art/design department.

On my first day, the BPPR's CEO explained my number one major responsibility on the job was to develop a strategy and execute the roll out and management of the crisis communication plan for the financial institution. The crisis could jeopardize the institution's reputation, assets, and the communities' well-being served for over 110 years. I worked side by side with the chief executive officer (CEO), the legal team, and the Washington-New York-based counsel. The nature of the crisis plan consisted of effectively communicating the USDOJ federal charges and agreements reached regarding the money laundering accusation impacting the institution. As the oldest and most important financial institution in Puerto Rico, US Virgin Islands, and the British Virgin Islands, synchronized readiness was imperative with clear measurable objectives, messaging, and open lines of communication.

When 9/11 happened, the United States responded with all its military might to protect against known/unknown foreign enemies who killed thousands that day. Money laundering was identified as a way to weave into USA everyday life. We experienced this with a client in San Juan but prior to 9/11, it was not detected. International and domestic banks weak points were attacked. Puerto Rico, though a US unincorporated territory, was found to be used as a money laundering point.

This case was extremely challenging and my previous experience proved immensely valuable as I was able to analyze and anticipate potential solutions. Research, pre-work, ideation, strategy mapping, and collaboration were extensive at all levels with its nuances and content. Corporate "go ahead" depended on USDOJ negotiated legal decisions/agreements. Changes and imposed restrictions forced us to reshape and adapt the communication strategy—both internal and external, local and stateside. Ethical principles were constantly monitored and applied to the communication strategy. Working hand in hand with the team proved to be a once-in-a-lifetime experience and opportunity. Finally, the institution entered into an agreement by signing a "one-year-silence non-disclosure clause ending in January 2004." It also rolled out financial federal safety prevention standards through education, supervision, processes, and robust employee training. Managing this crisis positioned me as an even more ethical PR professional because of the uniqueness with the case as this situation was a first in Puerto Rico.

After completing the federally imposed one-year silence, the bank went through a corporate change management restructuring and developed a new technology-based business, Evertec. I led its communication strategy and execution, involving new responsibilities for the new bank president's communication role.

Soon after this, another crisis brewed in a different financial institution. I was well known and my assets—strong in crisis communication and strategic management expertise—were required. It led me to develop and execute Doral's (DFC) strategic communication plan for its financial debt restructuring and recapitalization process. As chief communications officer (CCO) and executive committee member reporting directly to the CEO, I executed/supervised the communications strategy for all its audiences.

INTROSPECTIVE

Professionally, I process each case with accuracy, cultural knowledge, critical thinking, and situational awareness based on the case or the company's individual needs. My life-long mentors' words are always in the background. I'm truthful and honest and always honor my Puerto Rican roots and identity. I do it aware of the positive impact it has on those around me. My clients, students, mentees, Fellows, and colleagues all learn from my strengths, the knowledge acquired over time, and the vision and perspective I bring as a Puerto Rican woman to the table, the C-Suite, the classroom, and the community. Once sitting at the table, you have to present initiatives firmly, in the belief that these will be heard.

As a diverse and inclusive woman by birth, language, and skin color, I know that I belong right where I am professionally and individually. I share a unique perspective that not everyone understands. It may be more comfortable to stay within known walls, however, as a successful Puerto Rican professional woman in public relations, I understand emotions, what others just like me may experience, and what I may offer to complement with my strategic perspective richness. I have a vast heritage and mindset with a proven capacity to analyze and define commonalities in audiences and points of view in communication strategies. It's my legacy! I own it and proved it in Hawaii, Virginia, Washington, DC, Puerto Rico, and Texas. Like a ceiba tree standing tall, balancing in its strong roots and branches aiming at the skies, I taught myself to meet challenges by rebuilding every day. The ceiba tree is known for its ability to withstand all climates and conditions.

Language, food, and music equal uniqueness. Each brings joy. When shared, I become one with you at least for a while! As a Puerto Rican woman, I have it within me; I sincerely and thoughtfully share these gifts every time. In doing so, I'm grateful and honor my mother's and grandmother's wisdom and values, my sisters, aunts, sister-friends, and all the women in my life—past, present and future. I'm grateful to every one of them, and to you too, reader, who I am meeting today! Let me be your inspiration as you have inspired me so many times before.

That is what Latinas in PR have in common, we not only bring our professional experience into our field, but our diverse cultural experience as well. Together, let's find out what makes us ONE, what UNITES US, and what makes us LEARN, GROW, RESPECT, and SHARE! Let's advocate and be thankful for our "Latina-ness" and "Puerto Rican-ness" by giving voice and hope to the voiceless. We're ready, and we're empowered. *Bendiciones y gracias* (blessings and thanks).

MY VISIBILITY MOMENT

In reminiscing, I encountered my VISIBILITY moment upon my return to PR! My career's highest peak was in 1997 through 2008. I owned my moment, strengthened by my validated professional identity, capacity, and knowledge. I knew my worth. It was proven beyond a doubt. My international, state, and federal experience led me to advise top-level industry CEOs with ethical standards. I contributed to local communities' improvements; averted health, environmental, economic, and financial disasters; and provided tools to educate and improve health conditions in underprivileged areas.

Intention and assertiveness led me. I knew everything I learned through Old Dominion University's MA International Studies, my military wife's relocation experiences starting from zero, challenges and cultural exposures, racial and social disparities, and career achievements—it all merged to a point where I was empowered and felt it all as in a starburst, owning my moment and earning visibility. I was assertive, productive, and successful; I knew it. As a thorough strategic thinker, I could anticipate issues' cultural impact, prepare, validate, recommend, and avert chaos. I was determined, accountable, and decisive; I could lead, and I did. Each of these challenges were lessons met with patience, perseverance, and persistence. My experience was visible then as it is now! I reach out, give, and engage with the truth and sincere trust.

BIOGRAPHY

Olga Mayoral Wilson, MA, APR, Fellow PRSA, is an active crisis communications strategist who maintains open links with international clients in need of advice. Born and raised in Ponce, Puerto Rico, with a passion for learning, she earned two master's degrees: Strategic Communication at Texas State University and International Studies at Old Dominion University.

Olga's professional credentials include PRSA Fellow in 2014 and PRSA APR in 1983. Olga is also a service leader who collaborates with PRSSA Annual LATAM Student Competition's jury; PRSA Mentor/Mentee Program, Foundation's Scholarships Selection Committee; PRSA Foundation's Mentorship Initiative; PRSA National DEI Committee; COF Executive Committee (former Vice Chair and Secretary-Treasurer), COF Selection Committee, Good Fellow; COF Strategic Development Plan Sub-committee, and the PRSA UAB. Throughout her career and studies, she has always given thanks to her mentors, Mario Benitez, her first boss, and Fernando Valverde, APR, Fellow PRSA, who impacted her career the most and led her to success.

Olga also served as Senior Vice President and PR/Corporate Division manager of Banco Popular de Puerto Rico. Olga spearheaded communications inclusive of reputational crisis management (2002-2006), and 110-year celebration.

Following her volunteer instincts to serve diverse, inclusive, and underserved communities, she co-led communication and development efforts at Texas State University for Puntos de Vista

Spanish-Language International Festival for five years (2009-2013). Olga also coordinated the Hachar Media Professionals Program held annually during the School of Journalism and Mass Communications (SJMC)'s Mass Comm Week. In San Antonio, Texas, Olga volunteered for over nine years with the Puerto Rican Heritage Society developing the cultural events' communications strategy.

Olga retired after ten years as a senior lecturer from SJMC, Texas State University. She continues actively involved in mentoring young PR professionals through PRSA, and the College of Fellows.

Olga Mayoral Wilson, MA, APR, Fellow PRSA
X: @OlgaMWilson
LinkedIn: Olga Mayoral Wilson

THE KEY TO COMMUNICATION: BE A STORYTELLER!

MELISSA MONROE-YOUNG, MA, APR

"The world is huge, and while you can't be an expert at all the cultural nuances, you must be open-minded."

What is your story? Have you been neglected, abused, loved, or felt suicidal? How did you fight your way back to keep moving forward?

For me, storytelling became a way of life. It helped me overcome my "victim" status and understand that life is ripe with mountains that we must learn to climb. I knew I was meant to be in the communication business from an early age. As a kid, I would leave short stories all over the house. I always kept journals. And I remember my dad would tell me that the Black woman on TV anchoring the news would be me one day. Yes, that's right, my dad is African American, and my mom was proud to be Mexican American (she would often say Mexicana—her family didn't use Latina/o/x).

MY STORY

Growing up multiracial and moving from California to Texas as a teenager meant I had to deal with stereotypes, bias, and finding how to be comfortable in my own skin. Sometimes I call myself AfroLatina. Another day, I might call myself the old-school word "mixed." I even called myself Blaxican, but I've learned to be flexible and understand that different generations have their perceptions of what a multiracial person is. I remember someone telling me the word "mixed" wasn't preferred anymore, which is fine; but context and your audience matter.

I ventured into journalism to help people tell their stories and their truths. My story began in a loving home that was conflicted emotionally. In college, I chose to stop being a victim of my circumstances and move forward. I've experienced abuse, being poor, middle-income, homeless, and being back to middle-income. I wouldn't trade my experiences with anyone else.

While my personal story is worth sharing, it's not uncommon. I've heard some tear-jerking stories in my years as a journalist. Once, when covering the community beat, I interviewed a daughter and mom about being migrant workers and following the crops. As the daughter translated for her mom, who spoke Spanish, I was trying hard not to look at the basketball-sized hole in their living room floor, which showed the dirt from the ground. To them, that was home!

Now that both my parents have passed on, I learned they, too, were trying to work out their own identities or ego issues and gave my brother and me the best they had. My father taught me because of my race, ethnicity, and gender, I would always have to be a step ahead. My mother provided love, laughter, and emotional drama; life with her was a rollercoaster.

LEARNING TO BE A STORYTELLER

When I entered business journalism in the late 1990s, there was a resurgence in hiring Black and Brown employees. My internships with the National Association of Black Journalists (NABJ) helped me to land my first job with the San Antonio Business Journal. If it weren't for NABJ, I wouldn't be where I am today. But like the community beat, business journalism had its own set of unique skills. I didn't have that "killer" mindset as some of my colleagues did—so I got to work!

I often overworked myself to produce many stories so I wouldn't be seen as less than. I didn't crack jokes, have all the latest sarcasm, or could rattle off the balance sheet of a public company. But I hustled! I wasn't going to let my gender, being multiracial, or my lack of knowledge get in the way of someone telling me I wasn't good enough. My father's advice that I would have to work harder to get ahead never went away. And I did just that—hustled to prove myself.

I remember the BEST advice I received from an editor was read everything I could. Read the newspaper. Read magazines. Read how other journalists formed sentences and how they hooked the reader with repetition. From then on, my stories started to get better and required fewer edits. I stopped trying to be perfect and focused on being a storyteller.

Through being a journalist, ghostwriter, and public relations (PR) pro, I've learned that if you can humble yourself enough to talk with anyone, they are willing to share their story with you. When you listen and find their story, your media/press release becomes stronger, your blog post grabs the reader's attention, and your news story might be worthy of an award. Don't be satisfied with mediocre stories. Find that nugget of gold. One of my editors used to say, "Find the conflict."

The trigger questions that often get people talking are: What kind of hobbies do you have? Do you have children? What's the best restaurant you have been to? Do you have a dog or cat? Nowadays, people treat pets like their children and will shower you with pictures.

Despite what you learned in journalism or PR classes, not everything is strategic or a great story. Sometimes, you just need to churn things out to get the job done. Often, just being an active observer is enough.

As a PR professional, the story I pitched to the media about one of my best friends being a Black kidney donor to a stranger was easily picked up. I was an observer of her journey. She would send me short videos to post on social media for a group we are both a part of. To add to the post, I would research statistics on kidney disease. So, when it came time for me to chat with the reporter about her story, it was easy because I was an active observer.

PRACTICE AND EDIT

To my young communication friends, you must hone your storytelling gifts. That starts with the basics of writing and reading. While I went to journalism school and took English classes, I'm still not an expert on grammar rules. Thank God for Grammarly and AI grammar tools, but these are just tools that can often turn a great story into something void of emotion because they're trying to be too correct.

For example, I'm an editor for many Afro-centric articles, and often writers will use slang to express something. As a writer, you have to know when to be authentic and how not to be offensive—and that, my friends, takes practice.

No one wants to read a dull media release or a boring news article. Learn what makes your content stand out from the rest. Did a person defy all the odds to be in their role? Did the organization become the first in the state or nation to build the innovative widget? Everyone always thinks their news is the greatest, but it is your job to have that analytical eye to find the nugget of gold. And sometimes that wow factor is not always there. That's okay, too! Knowing you have to settle for less is being realistic. Toxic positivity from superiors can be frustrating when you don't have the information to deliver the goods.

Constant writing will force you to get faster and better. Write for your college newspaper, digital magazine, or blog. If that's not available, blog for your church. Don't go to church? That's fine, too. Do you have a friend who has a small business and could use help setting up and writing a blog? No excuses. Get writing!

MENTORS OR SIMILAR

Many of my editors served as my mentors—though they may not have realized it. It's important in this field to know your strengths and weaknesses and be honest with yourself. It's also important to understand that some mentors are just there for moments in time.

I didn't always agree with the editing style of some of my editors, who wanted to change every other word or would use big words that I didn't know the meaning of. I thought my readers wouldn't have a clue as well. An extensive vocabulary is ideal, but if the story is not understandable by all, you missed the mark. But I still learned from those "mentors" what I would accept and not accept as a writing style.

Nowadays, I don't have a mentor and, while I have a lot of experience, I still ask my colleagues for feedback and recommendations when necessary.

DEI MAKES WORLDLY SENSE

Communication goes hand in hand with diversity, equity, and inclusion (DEI) or similar terminology in your workplace.

You can't be a great storyteller or communicator if you are not willing to learn about a variety of voices.

The world is huge, and while you can't be an expert at all the cultural nuances, you must be open-minded. While skin color reveals a lot about a person, there are also invisible differences, such as being a part of the LGBTQ community, being a particular religion, or being a certain income level. These are also important factors that make people different.

I was pushed to be a DEI advocate when I wasn't quite ready for it. My father didn't teach us much about his race, even though we listened to Motown, rhythm and blues (R&B), and hip-hop music growing up. My African American father has his roots in the Black Creole culture. In this culture, it's easy to be "white passing" or blend in due to having a lighter skin color. For many Black Creoles, the brunt of racism is not as severe compared to darker-skinned Black folk. Most of the education I got about racism and colonialism, came from my own exploration and life experiences.

For instance, I remember during my internship in Harrisburg, Pennsylvania, I had just gotten paid and was happy. I took my cash to a beauty salon in the area, and the person there told me they didn't cut my hair type. She instructed me to go to the "other side" of town, which was basically the "hood," to get my hair "done." At the time, I didn't get the injustice in that situation until I got a bit older.

Another instance came years later when a reader called me upset about my Holy Week tourism story, which I was really proud of because it made 1A (front page) of the newspaper. She explained to me that using the word "Mexican" in the article was racist. The story was about people from Mexico shopping in San Antonio during the Holy Week vacation. She told me "Hispanic" was the preferred word. I was confused because I grew up with a mother who proudly said she was Mexican. It's interesting how society will manipulate us into thinking something is bad.

In 1998, another journalist and I founded the San Antonio Association of Black Journalists. I became an advocate in my newsroom for Black voices while trying to find my own voice. At another organization where I worked, I was also asked to be the Black advocate again. I think I was an easy "Black advocate target" since they knew I was in the communication field and could easily talk with anyone—white, Black, Brown, etc.

I find in many workspaces that silent bias is just as bad as blatant racism. Many organizations were quick to say they stood with the Black community when George Floyd died. Yet, they did little to advance Black and Brown communities and weren't actively hiring a truly diverse workforce. Now, many companies are walking back their DEI progress, even though the customers they serve are becoming more diverse, international, and gender neutral. This is mind-boggling to me because many economists will tell you the United States is becoming more of an international mecca. So, instead of educating our workforce on cultural awareness to help with customer service, we are bowing down to political pressure.

Friends: keep pushing and don't be afraid to be an advocate. You need a team of diverse people of skin color, gender, and age to appeal to the masses.

WORK ETHIC

A career in communications—whether journalism or PR—is still one of the best fields to be in and is ripe with opportunity despite artificial intelligence (AI). Yes, AI is here to stay but use it as a tool and be a critical thinker of it. You will often find me working late at night editing, writing, creating, grading—hustling! That's one of the beauties of this field: no one can take away your voice or ability to write and tell a story. In this field, you can be a full-time employee, part-timer, freelancer, or just volunteering for a nonprofit. A career in communication allows you to call the shots when you want to go fast or slow. Find that story for your organization, client, or yourself. Everyone has a story!

One thing to always remember is that your work ethic and humility will take you far. Many years ago, an editor gave me a chance when my writing ability was less than stellar, but I worked hard to prove myself.

VISIBILITY MOMENT

For many years, one of the things I took pride in was/is my work ethic. My colleagues knew I hustled, met deadlines, and didn't shy away from a little hard work. But as I won awards and received accolades, I also didn't learn the art of tooting my own horn.

Maybe it's culture or the pride I learned from my mom not to be boisterous. Staying quiet is not always a winning recipe. While I learned along the way to be an advocate for others, I didn't learn how to be an advocate for myself. I'm grateful for friends and colleagues who have seen my worth and felt the need to elevate me. One of my favorite quotes is from the 2011 movie, *The Help*. It goes, "You is smart, you is kind, you is important."

Advocating for yourself is a balancing act. My worth is not determined by titles, awards, my spouse, family, colleagues or employer but by ME! What makes me happy is determined by me. Yes, you have to make enough money to live, pay bills, have savings, and beyond, but you must enjoy your work and know it's not the end all, be all.

Think about what legacy you would like to leave when you are no longer on this earth and have fun on that journey creating that legacy. Then when you get a chance . . . toot that horn!

BIOGRAPHY

Melissa Monroe-Young, MA, APR, is an award-winning journalist and PR professional in San Antonio. She received a bachelor's degree from Texas Woman's University and a master's degree from Our Lady of the Lake University.

Before venturing into public relations, Melissa started her career mostly as a business journalist, working for a few different outlets. She had the opportunity to co-own a writing business and freelance for national and local magazines.

Melissa is a co-founder of the San Antonio Association of Black Journalists, which annually gives scholarships to communication students. She's also held several board roles with the San Antonio chapter of the Public Relations Society of America.

Melissa enjoys giving back to the community as a member of the San Antonio Chapter of The Links, Incorporated. She stays busy with her two teenagers, MJ and Meena, and her husband, Maurice. Amidst the chaos of life, Melissa always finds time to exercise and find some "me" time.

Melissa Monroe-Young, MA, APR
LinkedIn: Melissa Monroe

FROM TEEN MOM TO PR PRO

LORENA "LORRAINE" PULIDO, PHD

———————

"All of my efforts seemed in vain once I discovered I was going to become a teen mom—another likely statistic. But ultimately, my conviction and ambition catapulted me to pursue my studies with increased fervor."

As tears welled up in my eyes, I thought my future was over when the doctor handed me a positive pregnancy test at the age of sixteen. I was only a junior in high school and had my whole life mapped out until I saw that test result.

Just a few years before, when I entered Harlandale High School, I was hell-bent on becoming valedictorian. I followed the honors track, studied arduously, competed in the Academic Decathlon, secured leadership positions in the Student Council and other organizations, and pursued straight A's as if it were a sport. I even took drama classes and joined the drama club to increase my confidence as a public speaker. I was selected to join the drama University Interscholastic League (UIL) team and was recognized with All-Star Cast Honorable Mention honors.

Little did I realize that my drama class would do more for me than I could ever have anticipated. Not only did I become very comfortable performing in front of an audience, but I also became a leader, team player, troubleshooter, and chaos coordinator. So many of the experiences and skills I acquired in high school and later college would be essential to a future career I hadn't even recognized or fathomed—public relations (PR).

I initially had my heart set on a future career in journalism because of my genuine curiosity, empathy, love of storytelling, and written and oral communication skills. I joined the newspaper and yearbook staff to hone my journalistic talent. I even competed in the UIL competition for feature writing, and I won first place!

All of my efforts seemed in vain once I discovered I was going to become a teen mom—another likely statistic. But ultimately, my conviction and ambition catapulted me to pursue my studies with increased fervor. I gave birth to my daughter the first week of my senior year in high school after marrying her father that summer. I jumped right back into my honors curriculum, activities, and college applications, and was accepted to several selective universities.

After graduation, I went to an Ivy League university, the University of Pennsylvania, where I majored in English and minored in Spanish. I then earned my master's in journalism from the number one journalism school in the country, Columbia University Graduate School of Journalism. I was finally ready to enter the world of journalism. However, the job market in my hometown of San Antonio looked grim. I was pounding the pavement, but no one would open the door to opportunity. So, I accepted internships at a TV station, a bilingual newspaper, and a Spanish-language TV station.

Due to sheer necessity, I had to pivot from journalism to another field. I was disappointed that I couldn't find a job in journalism, after earning two Ivy League university degrees. I found myself skimming the want ads in the newspaper and was relieved to stumble upon one for a media relations coordinator at the University Health System (UHS). I read the qualifications—they all described me. I applied and I was hired for the position.

That was the genesis of my intense love affair with all things communications. Later, I became a part-time journalism adjunct instructor position at the same university where I pursued my PhD in Business and Leadership Studies—Our Lady of the Lake University. I continued working a full-time job while teaching. I loved it and moved on to teach PR at the University of Texas at San Antonio (UTSA), Palo Alto College (PAC), and now at Texas A&M University-San Antonio.

EXPANDING INTO TEACHING

In the last twenty-four years of teaching part-time, I've learned so much from my students. For example, I discovered, embraced, and championed social media as a powerful communication tool that can make or break a business based on their interest in the tools.

I understand my students and community well because I care how I may impact and influence future PR professionals in my care. Many of my former students remain in contact with me, and I have the privilege of seeing them fulfill their career aspirations. I've even hired some of my former students to work with me!

I'm blessed to teach a large percentage of non-traditional students, many of whom are balancing parenthood with their status as students and even as employees. I can relate to them because I was a teen mom who juggled being a student through my high school and college years. As a student, mom, and employee, I wholly empathize with my students' challenges, and practice grace and compassion to help ensure they thrive in my class.

COMBAT PROFESSIONAL LIMITATIONS

As a Latina in this industry, I have the opportunity to share a unique perspective that comes from my culture, heritage, and special upbringing, especially in San Antonio, where 60 percent of the population is Latino. Many of our PR target audiences are Latinos. Because of this, when I work with an agency or company targeting the Hispanic community, I'm poised to contribute effective and relevant strategies.

There is one particular disadvantage that many Hispanics face, though, and it's important to recognize and address it because it could be a detriment to progress. It is when a company pigeonholes a Latino communications professional into the sole role of marketing to only Hispanics, even when they are experienced in targeting other specialty markets and/or the general market.

This has happened to me. Yes, I'm 100 percent knowledgeable in the Latino community, the general market, and the bilingual community. Being bilingual has made me stand out when competing for a job, especially in cities with large Hispanic communities. But I have valuable experience in the general market target, too.

PR CAN MAKE CHANGE

Public relations is special to me because it's intrinsically rewarding. I've been able to help increase awareness and influence positive change in my community, thanks in large part to well-executed PR plans, whether it was helping to increase the number of people receiving their flu shots or the number of children enrolling at the San Antonio Independent School District, or the number of riders using VIA Metropolitan Transit's VIA Link or U-Pass. Through PR, I make a positive difference and am a change agent. I've seen my PR colleagues work in areas where their strategies can help save lives. They are increasing awareness of the importance of vaccinations or other health-related news items that can be the reason someone lives. What a blessing to make a living doing something I enjoy and love, and which others appreciate.

I've also used my PR expertise to better navigate my service on several boards, including the Alamo Colleges and Brooks Authority Boards, where I have a role in developing and implementing policies and initiatives, and guiding how our key messages are shared with our diverse stakeholders.

Undeniably, the biggest curveball that I and other PR professionals faced during our careers was the global COVID-19 pandemic. No one could anticipate how it would rock our world with death, sickness, mental anguish, job losses, food uncertainty, and lack of faith. Public relations professionals had to pivot to help their organizations survive. It was uncharted territory, with no true precedent during our lifetimes.

At VIA Metropolitan Transit, the government transit agency where I worked during the pandemic, we adjusted service and shared updates daily. Many people in our San Antonio community relied on us for their livelihoods. They needed VIA for their connection to employment, school, grocery stores, and healthcare, especially. Still, our bus operators and maintenance team members were also suffering from COVID-19, particularly before the vaccinations existed.

I learned to appreciate life and how fragile and unpredictable it can be. I learned how PR also helped uplift our community when it was in most dire need. I learned compassion, grace, and patience. My heart and faith grew thanks to overcoming these outrageous challenges.

Thanks to teamwork among media, PR professionals, our community, and our leaders, the insurmountable barriers were overcome. By working together to increase awareness and share calls to action, we overcame a time in our history that will never be forgotten.

LOOKING FORWARD AND SUPPORTING THE FUTURE

Our Latina community, especially in San Antonio, is rich in diversity. This represents an opportunity to further our footprint. I see our impact as strong and relevant to the general market community. Latinos are helping shape the future of PR by mentoring aspiring PR professionals.

Today, I serve as an adjunct communications professor and am actively teaching the profession to many prospective PR professionals. I share my experiences and explain how public relations can change the world by influencing public opinion and action.

When we review the chapters in our PR textbook, our class discussions can be quite engaging. Students become very involved and enthusiastic as they realize and appreciate the power of PR inside and outside their life experiences. Many of my students have selected PR as their career and have indicated that my class introduced them and convinced them to embark on this journey in the world of public relations.

Through my trajectory as a Latina PR professional, I must

inspire the next generation by sharing my personal insights and experiences with others. Women and Latinas can see themselves as future PR professionals when they see themselves represented. Representation truly matters.

As I reflect on how far I've come from teen mom to PR pro, the most valuable lesson I have learned through my thirty years of PR experience is to nurture your relationships because they are only as good as your last interaction. This is true in business and in life. You must invest time, genuine interest, and sweat equity in mutually beneficial relationships. In life, it took a tribe of college friends to support me and help me reach the finish line. In business, it has taken mentors, colleagues, and friends to help me move forward in my PR career.

I will continue to focus on public engagement for the betterment of our community and society. My sense of fulfillment comes from helping our organizations secure support for initiatives and programs, being of service to others who have a similar goal or desire by setting an example of what an ethical and tenacious PR professional should be, and demonstrating effective PR strategic thinking and influencing the future.

VISIBILITY MOMENT

As I reflect on my career, I remember vividly when I took the challenging step of starting my own PR consulting business. It was imperative that I get out of my comfort zone and actually implement a PR plan for my own business! Strategic networking and securing key connections were a necessity if I wanted to make a living practicing PR. In a competitive local market, I knew I had to actively reach out to people who knew my work. I contacted former employers and clients and let them know I was open for business. They either hired me or referred me to someone who could.

With every presentation in the pursuit of a new client, and with the sharing of well-thought-out ideas, the demand for my services increased. As a result, my self-confidence grew, my network expanded, and profit followed. It was so important that I believed in myself because if I couldn't, how could I expect others to do so? Taking that chance made me a better leader in so many ways.

BIOGRAPHY

Dr. Lorena "Lorraine" Pulido contributes her experience, expertise, heart, and soul to the causes she champions, including education, economic development, and transportation. She became the communications director for the San Antonio Independent School District (SAISD) in August 2024. She has thirty years of experience in the communications industry, previously serving as communications manager for VIA Metropolitan Transit and public relations manager for the City of San Antonio. She was elected the first female and first Latina chairperson to lead the Brooks Development Authority Board of Directors and as a trustee for Alamo Colleges District for District 4 in San Antonio, Texas.

She advocates for all students, especially those juggling parenthood and academics. She was a teen mom who took her daughter with her to the University of Pennsylvania, where she received her bachelor's degree. Later, she earned a master's degree from the Columbia University School of Journalism and a PhD from Our Lady of the Lake University. She is an award-winning PR professional and adjunct professor at Texas A&M University-San Antonio and has taught hundreds of students in her twenty-four years of teaching at various colleges. She was inducted into the San Antonio Women's Hall of Fame in 2023 and the Harlandale Independent School District Hall of Fame in 2021.

Lorena "Lorraine" Pulido, PhD
LinkedIn: Lorraine Pulido

WRITE AND REWRITE YOUR OWN STORY

IRASEMA ROMERO

"Coming home to the place I was born was exactly what I needed to meet and embrace more parts of myself."

I chose my career in public relations (PR) the summer before my senior year in high school. The main character in an ABC Family movie was a restaurant publicist, and I knew as I watched that I wanted an exciting career like hers.

My family immigrated to Texas from Mexico when I was ten years old, and my ambitions were as big as my parents' sacrifices. Every night, we would sit around the dinner table and discuss our plans for the future. I'd go to college, earn a degree in communications, and have a hugely successful career as a publicist in New York City.

As a teenager, I didn't question whether or not this was a

long shot. I believed it would happen. Decades later, I'm proud to say I've had an exciting fifteen-year career as a communications advisor. However, my experience looked a little different than I imagined as a West Mesquite High School senior, and I'm grateful for that.

OWNING YOUR STORY

I'm the oldest and only daughter in my family. When I graduated high school, I was adamant about moving away and joining my friends at the University of North Texas. I'd been accepted, had a scholarship ready, and I felt the pressure to demonstrate I could make it on my own.

On the other hand, my Mexican parents thought I was too young and weren't as excited by the idea of their seventeen-year-old daughter moving away. After a few heated arguments at the kitchen table, I ended up enrolling at a nearby community college in Dallas. Years later, I recognize staying home and saving money was a blessing in the long run, both financially and emotionally.

For the entire first semester, my dad drove me to college every morning on his way to work because I was afraid of driving on the freeway. I was afraid of a lot of things back then. Most of all, I worried about making the wrong move.

Two years later, with my associate's degree in hand, I was ready to move 1,200 miles away to Brigham Young University in Provo, Utah. I'd never even visited Utah. It was an opportunity to see and experience the world from a completely different perspective. For the first time in my life, I had to articulate my story as a Mexican immigrant when classmates and new friends asked, "Where are you from?"

"I'm originally from Mexico, but I grew up in Dallas," was my standard response. I felt the need to reassure the mostly-white audience that while I was born in Mexico, I was not from Mexico.

It made no difference to them. The usual response was, "Wow, you don't have an accent." I felt a sigh of relief at the comment, even as I held my breath. I was accepted, but did I truly belong here?

A couple of years later I moved to New York City (NYC) for a summer internship at a boutique PR agency in Midtown Manhattan. I was twenty-one years old and still remember the energy and excitement in the taxi ride from Newark Airport to the Upper West Side. Everyone belongs in the city of dreams. I was the main character in my own movie, with new possibilities and MIKA's "Grace Kelly" playing in the background.

During my time in NYC, I lived at the International House near Columbia's campus. Walking around the neighborhood one day, I saw the sign, quite literally—a bronze plaque with the name of the building: Columbia University's Graduate School of Journalism. "I want to go there someday," I remember thinking to myself.

It was a bit of unintentional manifesting. After graduation, I must have visited their website at least once a week for a year to research programs and plan my return to NYC.

My desire to attend Columbia was entirely for me. It was not about impressing my parents or helping my siblings. I wanted to continue learning and challenging myself, surrounded by people who dreamed big and wanted to make a difference as journalists and writers.

When applying to their master's program in magazine writing, I had "the talk" with my parents. You know, the one where you share why you want to spend an insane amount of money on an Ivy League university they haven't even heard of before?

I was impressed and grateful when my dad, Salvador, sitting in his favorite chair and without missing a beat, said, "I'll help you pay for half."

My dad didn't question whether or not I belonged at Columbia. I hadn't even been accepted, and he was prepared to help me get there.

There's a quote from the father of Malala Yousafzai, the Pakistani education activist, that has always reminded me of my own father. When asked how he supported his daughter, he says, "Don't ask me what I did, ask me what I did not do. I didn't clip her wings."

No hesitation, no doubts. Month after month for several years after graduating from Columbia, my dad helped me pay off my student loans faster than I would have on my own.

Everyone's story is different. The good news is that (in most cases) we get to define how it progresses. We simply need to be open to consider new possibilities.

THE STRUGGLE LEADS TO GROWTH

I'm confident that having Columbia on my resume opened doors I didn't even know existed. AT&T was one of them—and it's exactly where I was meant to be, both personally and professionally.

In 2015, AT&T expanded its presence in Mexico by acquiring two local telecommunications companies. With a week's notice, I arrived in Mexico City to help establish and lead the corporate communications team.

I was born in Mexico City, and at the time my grandparents still lived in the state of Mexico. While I spent the first few months living out of the luxurious JW Marriott Hotel, my grandparents were thirty minutes away in what is considered one of the most dangerous cities in the region. The juxtaposition was not lost on me.

On day one of the integration, a group of about a dozen other AT&T leaders, each with their own area of expertise, arrived at the Iusacell offices in Polanco. It was all-hands-on-deck, and the first order of business was to define the corporate narrative around our investment strategy in Mexico ahead of a press tour to position our new chief executive officer (CEO) and the company's investments in the country. In 2015, the telecommunications market in Mexico was in many ways monopolized by a single player. AT&T was bullish about disrupting the market and giving customers better options and a faster 4G network.

It was an exciting time as we all rallied to engage with

our new colleagues and deliver on the integration. Given my role directly supporting and ghostwriting for our CEO—in both Spanish and English—I was often the youngest person in executive team meetings. I remember feeling out of my element and unsure of myself, but also hungry to show up and excited by the work.

Outside of those meetings, I struggled to adjust to the social aspects of Mexican business culture, where time management is more relaxed and relationship building takes priority over efficiency. As much as I wanted to belong in corporate America, it turns out I actually wasn't Mexican enough in this new environment. My American accent when speaking Spanish gave me away, and my new colleagues didn't hesitate to point it out. I spoke Spanish daily with my family, but business Spanish took a few weeks to come naturally.

Living in Mexico City for three years redefined my career. For years I'd been the only Latina in the room, and I struggled to show up authentically in both professional and educational settings because I didn't feel like I belonged. Coming home to the place I was born was exactly what I needed to meet and embrace more parts of myself.

I'm grateful for that season in my life because it allowed me to expand my perspective and take inventory of the various moments that led me to accept that I can be fully Mexican and fully American. There's no single box for me to fit into. That realization was freeing and changed how I showed up to life and work moving forward.

BE OPEN TO NEW DIRECTIONS

Employee communications was the undervalued step-sibling of PR when I started at AT&T in 2011. Then, I moved to Mexico and discovered the influence of a strategic internal communications function to engage employees as brand ambassadors.

AT&T acquired two relatively small telecommunications companies in Mexico, all within weeks of each other. For years, these two companies competed for a fraction of the market share the unrelenting incumbent player didn't hold. Now, we were asking them to come together as the new AT&T Mexico team to deliver on a bold vision that required the best of each of us.

Well, it's easier said than done. Change is uncomfortable, and we introduced new policies, reorganized entire departments, integrated systems, and networks, and moved to new offices all within the first year. Employee communications and engagement quickly became my favorite part of the work as I led a small but mighty internal communications team that wasn't afraid to push the envelope to support nearly 20,000 employees across the country.

As part of launching the AT&T brand in Mexico, we deployed an internal campaign called *Somos* AT&T to help employees leave behind their old company jerseys and instead join the new AT&T Mexico team. Later, we also introduced an internal news broadcast hosted by two AT&T colleagues who embodied the dynamic energy we wanted to inject into our communications.

My experience in Mexico opened my eyes to new ways of applying my PR background. Combining my love for storytelling with my interest in creating inclusive corporate environments gave new purpose and meaning to my work leading internal communications.

Today, employee communications is my area of expertise. I'm glad I was willing to explore new opportunities outside of what I imagined my career in PR should be. I found the best niche for me, and you can, too.

CREATE A WELL-ROUNDED LIFE

Being a first-generation Latina leader comes with a sense of responsibility to make an impact, support our community, and be an example for younger generations. In this journey, I've learned we can't pour into—or help—others from an empty cup.

As exciting as my career has been over the past fifteen-plus years, there were seasons when my health also suffered, given the pace of the work. I loved it, but I experienced hair loss and digestive issues due to internalized stress and anxiety. Admittedly, I didn't know how to deal with it, and self-care was not a part of my routine.

When I returned to Dallas after an exciting season in Mexico, work lacked its usual appeal, and I felt tired of everything. As the eldest daughter in a Mexican immigrant family, I experienced a type of burnout that required more than a weeklong vacation on the beach. I needed a full reset, and I decided to take a sabbatical.

In 2018, I spent the summer hiking in Utah. My soul needed that time in the mountains to connect with deeper parts of myself and my identity outside my career or education. Through this process, I no longer felt the need to go 100 miles an hour, being everything to everyone, and always striving for more out of self-imposed expectations.

For years, my parents shared that I had exceeded all of their expectations. *No nos debes nada, mija.* You don't owe us anything, they'd said, as if to remind me to find my own happiness. I finally listened and gave myself the permission to create a more well-rounded life.

Since moving to Utah in 2020, I've become an avid hiker, learned to ski at thirty-five years old, and I'm an outdoor advocate and ambassador with organizations like the American Hiking Society and Women Who Explore. My career leading internal communications for a growing artificial intelligence (AI) startup continues to be an exciting part of my life. Still, I'm now comfortable closing my laptop and heading for a hike up the canyon. Most days, work can wait until tomorrow.

VISIBILITY MOMENT

My first couple of years at AT&T were a learning experience. It was a large communications team, and I flew under the radar, given my introverted personality. In 2014, I was invited to a small skip-level lunch with Larry Solomon, the senior vice president of global communications. We went around the table introducing ourselves and our backgrounds. Given the setting, I felt comfortable sharing more about my experience as a Mexican immigrant and my time at Columbia.

That was a turning point for my career at AT&T. Larry recognized my potential, and months later, he called with a new opportunity. AT&T was acquiring a telecommunications company in Mexico, and within days, I flew to Mexico City to help lead and establish a corporate communications team. I was twenty-seven years old.

I think about that fateful lunch often. If I had lacked the courage to share my story, someone else may have been tapped for the opportunity to move to Mexico. The courage to show up authentically was hard to muster earlier in my career because my story differed greatly from everyone else's. It's a reminder that simple conversations can redirect our path in bigger ways than we may recognize in the moment.

BIOGRAPHY

Irasema Romero is a seasoned internal communication advisor and leadership coach. She partners with leaders to foster high-performing teams through engaging, mission-critical organizational communications and programs.

As a purpose-driven leader with fifteen years of experience, Irasema has supported C-level executives through periods of major transformation and growth, including international merger-and-acquisition events and leadership/organizational changes.

Currently, Irasema leads internal communications for Gong, a leading AI-powered revenue intelligence platform. She also has a leadership coaching practice, Ollin Growth, helping emerging leaders embrace growth.

Irasema joined AT&T's Corporate Communications team in 2011 and served in various leadership roles supporting senior executives across the company during her nine-year tenure. She was promoted to a director position at twenty-seven years old. Prior to her departure in 2020, she supported AT&T's efforts to promote competition in the Mexican telecommunications industry by positioning its network expansion and the launch of the AT&T brand in Mexico.

She also led employee communications at Ancestry, where she partnered with senior leaders to introduce a new product vision and strategy following the company's change in ownership.

Originally from Dallas, Irasema lives in Salt Lake City and enjoys hiking, skiing, and visiting national parks in and outside of Utah.

Irasema Romero

Instagram: @ollingrowth

LinkedIn: Irasema Romero

LEADING STARTS WITH YOUR MINDSET

PAOLA ANDREA VARGAS-STRASSNER, MPS, APR

"Commitment, perseverance, passion, and willingness to learn will open doors and take you where you want to be."

MEDIA AND PUBLIC AFFAIRS

The public relations (PR) industry is important as it spans any field, and when done right, it becomes invaluable. Being the public affairs officer (PAO) for a government organization is a great responsibility that I take proudly. As a bilingual Latina, I can provide added benefits that shape my work in public relations communications, especially when I am able to assist colleagues with communications messaging or products that reach out to the Spanish-speaking public and stakeholders we serve.

Furthermore, being a Latina can be an advantage or a disadvantage. As with any other ethnicity in any industry, it depends on what you want to accomplish, influenced by your own cultural acceptance, mindset, and outlook. How you see yourself and what you project to others can turn into a negative or a positive.

MAXIMIZE YOUR FULL POTENTIAL

Upon college graduation in 2004, I moved from Bogota, Colombia, to Orlando, Florida. A year later, I had my first professional opportunity with Azteca America TV, working as an account executive. I was initially interested in pursuing an audiovisual production role with Azteca. However, as a mid-size local station, the programming came from the network, so there was minimal local production. I embraced the challenge, took on the new role, and became a media consultant in advertising sales.

Through this opportunity, I met business owners and maximized my full potential to bring the capital needed for production. This is how I was able to work in pre-production, voice-overs, and as an entertainment reporter. I had my first English interview, aired to a Spanish-speaking audience, which I highlight as one of the many advantages of being a bilingual Latina. Some exciting work with Azteca included infomercials, bulletins, and events coverage. Working there was an important first step, where I learned more about the central Florida media market and built lasting professional relationships, earned visibility and increased station production.

Soon after, I had a radio opportunity to work behind the cameras in a more relaxed environment—one that requires equal preparation and discipline to meet scheduling and content programming. I was invited to participate as a guest in a show and ended up co-hosting *Pase la Tarde con Melodía*, a two-hour daily radio show in Radio *Melodía*—RCN Orlando—for the Colombian audience in central Florida who could tune in online or with a portable radio.

As I grew in the profession, I became a marketing manager with the first bilingual newspaper in Orlando, *El Osceola Star*, where I learned the power of networking and media relations. I had the pleasure to interview the first bilingual public information officer of St. Cloud, a Latina who strongly advocated to find unity among English and limited English proficient (LEP) speakers. After a delightful conversation with her, I knew I wanted to learn more about public affairs and get more involved with organizational communications.

At *El Osceola Star*, my former boss, Guillermo "Bill" Hansen, who is no longer with us and left a legacy within the Hispanic community in Florida, became my first mentor. He prepared me to participate in public relations, assisting the Hispanic members of the Kissimmee/Osceola Chamber of Commerce with event planning. As the marketing manager, I also wrote Spanish columns and translated from English to Spanish, and quickly realized I needed to be more than proficient in English. I had my bachelor's from Colombia but needed the specialized English terms for the profession, so I went to broadcasting school.

Commitment, perseverance, passion, and willingness to learn will open doors and take you where you want to be.

EMBRACE YOUR JOURNEY

When speaking to young Latinos and Latinas who have recently migrated to America, I remind them of the importance of keeping a long-term goal in mind and working towards it until you get there, and that there is not always a linear path. As an immigrant, you realize and understand that sometimes it could take double the time, effort, and flexibility to work those extra jobs that will pay the bills. At the same time, you get the certificate, license, or degree you need to become the professional you want in the industry you want to be, in this case, communications, media, and PR.

While some people build a career in a company and are happy with it, which is perfectly fine, I have been happy with my non-linear process because it has taught me to recognize my strengths and weaknesses. I firmly believe that you don't need to be a lifetime with a company to make a positive impact and drive change. I attribute part of my success to that way of thinking because I take every role and opportunity with professionalism, giving my best.

I am grateful to my parents for that because, as successful business owners, they raised me with the constant reminder that *"el tiempo es oro,"* or "time is golden," and I make sure I use it wisely. So do not be afraid of having a non-linear path. Instead, embrace your learning process and be open to the opportunities presented to you without forgetting your long-term goals.

Benjamin Franklin and Mae Jameson are two of my inspiring figures for being successful leaders with non-linear paths. Aside from being a founding father, Franklin was a diplomat, writer, scientist, salesman, inventor, and publisher, which defines him as a polymath, one of the best in history for embracing knowledge.

Similarly, Jameson, who is most known for being one of the African American NASA astronauts, is also a teacher, dancer, actress, doctor, engineer, and researcher, which I think is remarkable and fascinating at the same time. Franklin and Jameson knew and understood that time was of the essence and used it to do what they enjoyed without worrying about changing career paths. They knew they had made an impact with the positive changes needed, and it was time to embark on the next project needed at their time.

A non-linear path also can become a challenge because big companies need employee retention, and we all need those years of experience on our resumes for career growth. Also, some people need stability, so non-linear paths don't work for everyone, and you must do what works best for you.

One of the most important things for me was to become a mom, and when the time came, I managed a team at a flagship retail store in Carlsbad, California. I was responsible for high-volume sales and led a team of stylists in marketing, customer relations, and branding. While I was exceeding company goals, I also was experiencing my first pregnancy and wanted to take maternity leave to stay at home for the first five years.

The company I was working with was amazing. I had previously worked with them in Florida, Washington, DC, and California. As I relocated to Maryland after the birth, they offered me the opportunity to stay with them in another management position within the Maryland/DC area. Thinking about working during the holidays with a newborn made me realize that this was the time to reevaluate my future. Although I was grateful to the company for its support, it was time to cross the bridge and rethink my personal and professional goals.

Things worked well for me during my extended maternity leave, and I was able to enjoy the first five years as a stay-at-home mom with my beautiful family. I planned to rejoin the workforce once the girls were ready for daycare. I took on the virtual learning opportunity and became an interpreter, which gave me the flexibility to be at home with the girls. As a working mom, I felt productive and strengthened my English language skills. I started my application process in the communications and media industry, facing many obstacles at this point, mainly because of the maternity gap.

So, what do you do? I speak about this with many immigrants who have accomplished professional goals in their birth countries. Still, once they migrated, they had to start all over, with all that entails—sometimes passing as uneducated just because of the cultural differences or language barrier. Same with the stay-at-home moms, who willingly left their careers behind to raise a family, and once they felt ready to go back to work, they were either "overqualified" for the position or not compensated as they should have been, which was my case. Personally and professionally, things can only affect you to the extent you let them, so I didn't get discouraged.

At that pivotal time, I joined the Public Relations Society of America (PRSA) and made many powerful connections with like-minded professionals. I enjoyed volunteering at public relations events and have been an active member since then. Knowing I wanted to return to the media industry, I needed to freshen up my skills and continue learning. I got accepted into the Strategic Public Relations Master's program at George Washington University in Washington, DC, and completed my graduate degree while caring for my two little ones. It was a challenging time because of my responsibilities as a mom, so I had to become more organized and endure longer days.

During my final stretch in grad school, I got accepted into a Pathways Internship Program as a Public Affairs Student Trainee working full-time for a defense media government agency. Can you believe it?

I was extremely blessed, fortunate, and happy with that experience, which came at the perfect time when my daughters were just starting daycare, and my father's immigration petition had been accepted, so he was living with us. My family has been my support, and I especially thank my dad for the discipline, and my mom for the positivity and knowledge instilled in me during my journey.

SHAPING THE FUTURE OF PR

Some people want to see you thrive, be it your family, friends, or colleagues. Finding those who are rooting for you will help you grow and reach your goals. If you are a student, surround yourself with those who want to see you thrive. If you are interested in PR and communications, I can say that PRSA has been the foundation where I've found the right mentorship in my professional development and has helped me to be where I am today.

Through PRSA and the power of positive relations, I connected with a wonderful new mentor during an internship while finishing graduate school and became accredited in public relations (APR). Among the talented practitioners I've met, I also came across Melissa Vela-Williamson, who invited me to collaborate on this project to share our Latina journeys in hopes of inspiring you and others to achieve your goals and full potential through our personal and professional experiences in the communications and public relations industries.

Latinas are shaping the future of PR through our creative, multi-faceted work, which impacts different industries; just see the talented profiles compiled in this book. While we are all PR Latina practitioners, our fields differ across various regions, offering our organizations unique expertise.

As a public affairs officer, I see myself positively impacting Maryland and the youth we serve without thinking I am a Latina. I want to make an impact by knowing I am a part of my community and erasing any sort of label that can be divisive. It has been up to me to learn the skills I needed to learn to be where I am today, breaking barriers to become the trusted counselor I aspired to be when I entered the public affairs field.

Developing a growth mindset has helped me in my professional success, and I think it is relevant for the evolution of our society to combat some of the victim mentality that still prevails in some cultures. Yes, while systemic racism exists, the leaders who achieve their full potential solely focus on driving change.

Your cultural acceptance and mindset will determine your sense of belonging. Your thoughts dictate your actions, and your actions determine your future. Knowing that you are part of the community you are in and that you are of Hispanic descent is a plus; if you can speak Spanish, it is a bonus. Understanding that we communicate through language also means that to succeed, we need to become communications and language experts.

We can serve as PR practitioners and drive positive change by offering mutually beneficial relationships with ethical decisions. Shaping the future of Latinas in PR involves our confidence and ability to provide strategic advice, and we must deliver on that commitment so that the right compensation is part of the equation for what we bring to the table.

My aspirations for my future in public relations are to continue to grow as a public affairs leader, adapt to the ever-evolving digital media landscape and new technologies, and combat misinformation with accuracy and transparency. I am passing on knowledge and developing others through mentorship, as it has been passed on to me, empowering others to achieve their goals for success in this beautiful profession.

MY VISIBILITY MOMENT

Some steps in our journey are more joyful than others, especially when we realize that the effort and commitment we've put into something has finally paid off. For me, it was returning to the workforce after several years as a stay-at-home mom. I was planning to return to a communications and media role.

In doing so, I remembered that I had set my own goals, one of which was to work in communications in the English language. I had set that goal when I relocated from Florida to DC in 2008.

Ten years later, I finished a master's degree in strategic public relations at George Washington University and worked as a public affairs student trainee with Defense Media Activity. Looking back at that moment helped me regain clarity and a sense of purpose to establish new goals and to be thankful for the many things I had accomplished. At that point in time, I was discovering what life was like with kids. Grateful that I had found my new motivation, I became a professional working mom, on my way to completing graduate school, an internship, and earning my accreditation in PR.

BIOGRAPHY

Paola Andrea Vargas-Strassner is an accredited public affairs professional working for the state of Maryland. Born in Bogota, Colombia, she received her bachelor of arts degree in social communication and audiovisual production from the Pontifical Xavier University and a master's degree in strategic public relations from the George Washington University.

She joined Azteca America TV in 2005 as an account executive and entertainment reporter, opening the doors to trusted mid-size Hispanic networks in central Florida, such as Radio *Melodía*-RCN Orlando and *El Osceola Star* newspaper, that earned her early recognition for her media talents as DJ host, marketing manager, and staff writer.

Paola relocated to Washington, DC in 2008, where she gained nonprofit experience as a Hispanic media outreach volunteer for Atlas Corps. Her involvement with the community through volunteering and service roles includes the San Diego Colombian Chamber of Commerce as the secretary of the board of directors in 2011, the Girl Scouts of Central Maryland in 2022, and currently with the Public Relations Society of America, where she has been active since 2017.

As a Maryland resident, she has served as a strategic communications professional and interpreter, and enjoys spending time with her family while working in communications and public affairs.

Paola Andrea Vargas-Strassner, MPS, APR
LinkedIn: Paola Vargas-Strassner

FROM THE SONORAN DESERT TO SUCCESS: MY JOURNEY IN PUBLIC RELATIONS

MARISOL VINDIOLA

"If you are not seen, you are not known. If you are not known, you will not be recruited."

ROOTS IN RESILIENCE

I always dreamed of living authentically and making a difference in the world, even when life challenged me at every turn. "If life gives you lemons, make lemonade"—that's my motto. Growing up in a small town in Sonora, Mexico, I came from humble beginnings and lived a simple life. Our family was large—six siblings. We had endless adventures and fun times together. To this day, we laugh about our childhood experiences and how hard we had to work to get to where we are now.

My life wasn't always easy. When I was three or four years old, one of my earliest memories was smiling at my handsome doctor (*desde niña era coqueta, ahh*) while he touched my shaved head and checked my vital signs. I was hospitalized with a brain tumor and suffered through multiple lifesaving surgeries. It was a long road to recovery, with many months spent in a hospital, often connected to devices monitoring my head and tied to the bed to prevent their disconnection. But those challenges, tough as they were, instilled in me a profound appreciation, gratitude, and love for life.

THE GIFT OF FREEDOM

Now, there's nothing I cherish more than my freedom and the ability to truly enjoy every day. Those many months in the hospital shaped me, and I believe they're the reason I value my freedom so deeply. My most treasured possessions and values are resilience, love, and a passion for enjoying life's simple things. *Amo la libertad de ser yo misma, y como decía Frida Kahlo, "Pies, para qué los quiero si tengo alas para volar?"*

Of course, with that tough time came other problems. Our family faced financial and emotional storms. Imagine my beautiful mom, only twenty-seven years old, juggling six little kids while one fought for life in the hospital. It was a challenge, and though our journey wasn't easy, we learned resilience. My parents divorced due to alcoholism and domestic violence, and since my mom needed to work all day and later remarried, she couldn't take care of us. We were sent to live with our grandparents and relatives until further notice, which ended up being until I was eighteen.

MARISOL VINDIOLA

FINDING STABILITY

Growing up, we were back and forth between my mom's, aunts', and grandparents' homes, constantly moving and adjusting. We moved so many times—from houses, towns, and cities to different schools—that I lost count. This is why I became so adaptable, knowledgeable, and accepting of people from many places and backgrounds. My friends are amazed at my network from all over Mexico, Arizona, and the United States—especially from the Sonora region, across different social statuses, ages, and genders.

My siblings and I always ended up with our grandparents in a small town in the Río Sonora, Mexico basin. Some friends even joke, saying, *"Conoces hasta los perros callejeros"*—you even know the street dogs.

My grandparents and relatives were strict. They instilled a sense of responsibility and curiosity to keep learning and educating ourselves. Thanks to them, my siblings and I were always there for each other. We learned to swim in the river together, climb and slide on the hills and mountains, and harvest fruit like *membrillos, pitayas, granadas, limones,* and *duraznos* from my grandma's and neighbor's homes. My siblings and I always joke, saying we were fed organic food and didn't even realize it.

The Vindiola kids were known as some of the most intelligent students in school; even now, teachers use us as examples. Those are the memories I cherish most. To this day, my siblings are my best friends, and I know that no matter what life throws our way, we'll always have each other's backs. My sister

Dulce always defends me from everyone; perhaps that is why I don't know how to defend myself. She always did it for me. She is my best friend. From this, I learned how to have fun, be adventurous, care for others, and be kind and compassionate.

CHERISHED MEMORIES

I have so many fond memories of my grandpa taking us and our childhood friends, Lupita and Toñita, to his farm, or *La Milpa*. We would jump on top of dried bean or peanut plants to help him harvest, and he always ensured we were having fun while spending time together. It feels like yesterday that we were laughing together. Those were truly the best memories. My grandpa was a hardworking person who taught us to be smart with math, have an entrepreneurial spirit, and connect with nature. We would lie on the patio outside his house at night and gaze at the stars and planets. What a memory!

He always encouraged me to be a famous radio host or TV anchor because I asked so many questions and couldn't stop talking. Once, he was ready to go to sleep, but I didn't let him because I wanted him to keep telling me stories. And guess what? I now host a binational radio show called *Las Suculentas,* which is broadcast in Arizona and Sonora on three popular radio stations and a podcast. He truly saw my essence, even when he knew I was a very introverted and shy little girl who always tried not to be seen.

My grandpa passed away when I was eight years old, and my best friend, Toñita, also passed. These are some of the worst losses I've experienced and have never fully recovered from. I miss my grandpa every day, and I think about my friend at times, too. I truly believe he has been my guardian angel, always looking after me. After my grandpa passed away, we stayed under the care of my grandma, who was very strict. She made us go to church and attend mass every day and ensured we had good grades in school—nothing less than excellent. My grandma wasn't caring, but she always ensured we were doing well in school, as she loved reading and educating herself.

THE CHALLENGES OF GROWING UP

As a pre-teen, I was very timid and, believe it or not, quite introverted. My signature was a smile on my face, because: *"Una sonrisa puede abrirte muchas puertas."* I was private and reserved, only opening with my close circle where I felt safe. I started working with my mom at her little corner store and then at her bakery when I was eleven or twelve. I worked at my older sister Carmen's shop in La Sierra de Sonora when I was thirteen. I was always looking for something to do. This is where I learned to love work, customer service, connecting with people, and the value of hard work in earning money. For me, it was like playing while making money.

DISCOVERING MY VOICE

It wasn't until middle school, after so many moves, that I started being part of a group of friends besides my sisters. In high school, I did my social service in the school library, which helped me come out of my shell and become popular among my classmates. My sisters described me as selective in picking friends. I talked to everyone but wasn't close to many. I have always known what I wanted in life and only agreed to do what I truly enjoyed, nothing more. I have always been responsible, dedicated, and reliable. I love helping others and know what I want in life. Above all, I love connecting to people, being authentic, being in my own skin, and enjoying every single experience. I have always been that way and never plan to change. Being authentic and strong and having the certainty of knowing that everything will be fine is my superpower.

As a teenager, I spent hours reading, writing love poems, painting the vibrant colors of the majestic Sonoran Desert surroundings, riding horses and donkeys, and joining the high school orchestra and chorus—even though I wasn't a good singer. I just wanted to be part of something. During university, I enrolled in the women's baseball team, practiced weightlifting, and was one of two women boxers and boxing students in Hermosillo, Mexico. I became popular with friends, understood their conversations, and was unconventional in a closed and conventional society where girls were expected to be just pretty and well-behaved, and *"Calladita te ves más bonita."* My mom's and grandma's houses were the hubs for my friends to gather every night. By now, I knew that my passion was connecting with people and making a good impression, and that public relations (PR) was my best skill.

JUGGLING RESPONSIBILITIES

At the same time, I studied business administration at the University of Sonora in the mornings and worked part-time in a clothes boutique in the afternoons, evenings, and weekends. Then, I worked as an assistant to an assistant accountant for an engineering services mining company and later in marketing studies. I was good at accounting but realized it wasn't my thing; I loved PR and traveling. I tried to become a tourist guide in San Carlos, Mexico, but my mom didn't let me travel from Hermosillo to Guaymas, Sonora, every weekend. I also worked at DESEM (equivalent to Junior Achievement in the United States) in the statistics and PR departments. During college, my friends and I founded a startup where I served as the director of public relations. This role allowed me to travel throughout Mexico, presenting our project and networking with young entrepreneurs across Latin America.

EMBRACING CHANGE

Later, one of my best friends insisted I apply for a one-year scholarship to study English as a second language through the Arizona-Sonora Commission. We applied, and I was accepted. Against my mom's will, due to the financial situation, I moved to Tucson, Arizona, not knowing anyone and barely speaking any English. It was a tough and lonely time. I think I cried almost every day. But soon, I started meeting people from all over the world as an international student. Someone told me about the Consulate of Mexico in Tucson, where I offered my social service.

They offered me a job in the legal and public, and then in the media and PR departments. At twenty-two, I had my diplomatic visa as local staff of the Consulate of Mexico in Tucson, Arizona. My network expanded, and I was making money to support myself and help my family in Mexico. I worked there for three to four years.

By twenty-five, I was married and then had two kids, Andree and Ethan. However, the marriage was difficult, happiness eluded me, and I wasn't enjoying life. This wasn't me—not for me. It was another significant challenge to overcome. I separated when I was three months pregnant with my second child, who turned out to be twins. During my second pregnancy, I lost one of the twins, and depression hit me hard, throwing me to rock bottom. But I had no choice but to repress my postpartum depression and keep going. I had two babies now and needed to be even stronger than before. As a single mother without any support, I had to mature overnight. From that day forward, I worked and studied hard to ensure my two babies had everything they needed. We were the three musketeers. At the time, I was working at a well-known cell phone company in retention and customer services.

A NEW CHAPTER BEGINS

In 2008, I met a regular customer at the cell phone company. She was impressed with my customer service and sales skills and invited me to work at her office; as filmmaker Alejandro Jodorowsky said, *"Si dios te tira un dulce, abre la boca y cómetelo!"*

I was hired as an administrative assistant at Visit Tucson,

where I worked for over sixteen years in their Mexico Marketing Department. I moved up to coordinator, then manager of the department, then director of Mexico Initiatives, and finally, senior director of Multicultural Marketing. My role involved promoting our city as a destination in Mexico's primary market and the multicultural market in the United States and PR within the Hispanic community in Arizona and Mexico. I had the opportunity to learn about the amazing tourism and hospitality industry.

ACHIEVEMENTS AND RECOGNITION

During these years, I have met leaders in the industry at local, state, national, and international levels, been part of the tourism committee for the Arizona-Mexico Commission, and served as vice chair of Arizona Town Hall. I have been awarded for Best Public Relations Campaign by PRSA, Best Marketing Campaign by the Arizona Governor's Tourism Office, and recognized as an Inspirational Hispanic in the United States by ABC's *Good Morning America.* These accolades are some of the rewards for my journey and led me to my current position in business development with an Ad Tech company, allowing me to network with leaders in various industries from all over the United States, Mexico, and Latin America.

I now have my binational radio show, produce my own podcast, am a public speaker, and have many other accomplishments along the way. I now know that I have made it. I am living my dream, the famous American Dream! But the journey continues. My superpowers are being bilingual, binational, bicultural, Mexican, Sonorense, and a proud Latina. These and my attitude towards life have been key to my career and professional journey's success in tourism and PR.

Now it's your turn: Your superpower is to be a Latina in public relations.

MY VISIBILITY MOMENT

I have always been an advocate for promoting others— my friends, colleagues, clients, employers, and especially young Latinas and Latina entrepreneurs from the binational region. These efforts have created business opportunities and increased revenues for those I supported. However, it wasn't until I accepted leadership positions in local, national, and state tourism and PR, along with speaking engagements and awards, that the recognition I facilitated for others began to bring me personal advancements. These opportunities provided me with new resources, personal growth, and a deeper awareness of my own strengths and abilities.

Self-promotion doesn't come naturally to many Latina women, particularly in male-dominated or non-Latin spaces— but it's essential. I experienced firsthand how high-level national and state exposure transformed my career, opening doors to job offers and client opportunities that once seemed out of reach. If you are not seen, you are not known. If you are not known, you will not be recruited. My passion for multicultural representation in the PR and tourism industries can only be realized if I have a seat at the table, and visibility has given me that seat.

BIOGRAPHY

Marisol Vindiola is the Senior Business Development Manager of Orange 142 and former Senior Director of Multicultural Marketing at Visit Tucson. In her role at Visit Tucson, she oversaw all aspects of multicultural marketing within the cross-functional organization. This included visitor outreach, activities, business, and event planning, as well as assisting in United States/Mexico projects to accomplish organizational and departmental objectives. She also managed Visit Tucson's efforts to reach and engage diverse communities and drive cross-sector impact within the community. Additionally, she worked with all Visit Tucson departments, business partners, and local, state, and international governmental organizations to strengthen the promotion of Tucson, Arizona, in Mexico and within the Hispanic market in the United States.

Before joining Visit Tucson, Marisol served as the Public and Media Relations Coordinator for the Consulate of Mexico in Tucson. She also serves as an executive board member on the boards of directors for Arizona Town Hall, the Public Relations Society of America–Tucson Chapter, Tucson-Mexico Sister Cities, and is a member of the Arizona-Mexico Commission Tourism Committee. She hosts a binational radio show in Southern Arizona and Mexico and collaborates on writing articles related to tourism promotion for major Spanish-language media.

Marisol has been awarded for community service by the League of United Latin American Citizens (LULAC), for two

Best Public Relations Campaigns by PRSA in the Multicultural Communication Category, Best Marketing Campaign by the Arizona Governor's Tourism Office, and recognized as an Inspirational Hispanic in the United States by ABC's *Good Morning America* and a proclamation from Pima County Board of Supervisors for Hispanic Heritage Month. These accolades reflect her journey and have led her to her current position in business development with an Ad Tech company, allowing her to network with leaders in the tourism industries across the United States, Mexico, and Latin America.

Marisol holds a bachelor's degree in business administration from the Universidad de Sonora in Mexico. She also has certifications in digital marketing, nonprofit leadership and management, and a business certificate from the University of Arizona in Tucson, Arizona. She is originally from Sonora, Mexico, and resides in Tucson with her two sons, Andree and Ethan. Her superpowers include being bilingual, binational, bicultural, and a proud Latina.

Marisol Vindiola
Facebook: @Marisol Vindiola
Instagram: @MarisolVR17
X: @MarisolVindiola
LinkedIn: Marisol Vindiola

THE PATH TO SUCCESS ISN'T LINEAR

MELISSA VELA-WILLIAMSON, MA, APR, FELLOW PRSA, CDP

———

"The next generation may need to see you to one day be you. Leave a legacy worth following."

I have interviewed and connected with countless public relations (PR) leaders over the past two decades of PR and content creation work. Most of those leaders, especially those from Hispanic or Latino backgrounds, did not travel a smooth, straight path to their success. Many PR pros, including me, didn't major in PR in college. Some didn't even intend to work in the field!

Almost every time I ask one of my *Smart Talk Series* podcast guests to tell me how they got to where they are professionally, I learn that they did not follow a linear path. Many of us found our profession by happenstance or within the workplace. If that's your story, you must shift the narrative about how you got into PR from something that seems accidental to a path that was destined. Accidents make us feel out of control or like imposters. Destiny sounds ordained. Let's use our positioning know-how to benefit how we brand ourselves from the inside out! A non-linear career path is the norm. My career origin story proves that a straight path isn't necessary for success.

STARTING WITHOUT A MAP

For most first-generation college students, the journey through college is full of missteps. Without a guide or a path mapped out for me by my parents, making my way through college felt a lot like being a pioneer. I had to figure out my first steps, clear away thorny obstacles, and stumble through the unexpected all along the way.

Today, I am a PR strategist who feels at the top of her game. I have worked in all major sectors of PR, advised over one hundred brands, and written, spoken, or trained pros at all levels. I'm probably so accomplished in my work *because* I started my career inadequately. When I started in PR, I was enthusiastic but ignorant!

As the first in my family to attend a four-year university, I was intimidated by large campuses. So, I followed some friends to a local but private university. I realized how expensive that decision would be when I saw my first tuition bill!

As a student quickly accumulating loan debt, I was motivated to find a promising career path. Like many children, I had said I wanted to be a veterinarian when I grew up. My first long lab class as a freshman in college showed me that I didn't have the temperament (or stomach) for what *that* education would entail. By my second semester, I was back to trying to decide what my major should be. I needed to find an academic track that would lead me to a career lucrative enough to pay my loans off. At that point, all I knew about my career interests was that I was creative and had a knack for writing.

READING THE SIGNS

Sometimes, it's better to focus on the information we *do* have rather than focus on what we don't know. What I knew about my gifts as a young adult helped me find my way forward. I knew I had an eye for photography and excelled in every writing class I took.

By college, I was already a published writer, writing poetry and essays for outlets that ranged from student works to national publications. My first part-time jobs were in photography, but there were few opportunities to work full-time in it. Pragmatically, I knew that neither poetry nor photography offered a stable career path for me to pursue. My uncertainty made me a frequent visitor of Career Services—enrolling in their courses and pursuing their resources each semester. Surely, I could figure out how to use my communication skills, love of writing, and creative interests to help me find a career. Determining my route would be easier if I knew my destination!

I chose an English/Communication Arts major that had me dabble in a bit of everything. I was academically interested, but my view toward a career path was still murky. It took until the last semester of my senior year for me to find my way to PR. During a capstone class, students were required to research their prospective career roles and present their ideal job as the final project. The only role I could come up with after combining what I knew about my skills with viable career options was to be an advertising copywriter. I did my presentation on that role, and while that job did sound fun, it felt unrealistic as a viable prospect in my local area. My worries seemed to be preparing to graduate with me after all those years of exploration.

Luckily, a classmate named Kate presented her goal of working in PR. She shared about her recent internship in PR and how she helped a nonprofit earn media coverage about their work to equip people with disabilities to learn to water ski. That sounded purposeful and fun! Finally, my career goal was in sight. I could work in PR!

Before this class, I had completed a marketing internship at a local theme park. That work was entertaining, but it was unfulfilling. Promoting ticket sales left me wanting more—more connection or more purpose—I wasn't sure what I was looking for then. But when Kate described what she did in PR, using multiple communication disciplines to promote an event that changed lives, my destination became clear.

Public relations sounded creative, dynamic, purposeful, and important. I could work with photographers, write and publish with or through news outlets, and connect needs with resources. Plus, there were many more PR roles open than copywriter roles. This was the destination I was searching for!

As we finished our senior year, I got busy learning more about PR and trying to find someone who could lead me to a job opening. My mother had shown me countless times how useful it was to ask people for help. So, I started telling everyone I knew that my goal was to work in PR. That grassroots strategy helped me find my first PR opportunity and start in the field.

One day, I was talking with a spin instructor, Mario, at the gym about my plans after graduation. I shared how I just accepted a grant writing job at a tiny nonprofit but wasn't excited about starting.

"I don't really want to be a grant writer, but I need to start making money because my loan payments begin soon," I said. "Well, what do you want to do?" he asked. "I want to work in PR, but I can't find a job posting about it in the paper, and I don't know anyone who does that work," I said. "Huh," said Mario. "Didn't I tell you my wife co-owns a PR firm? You should call her. She hires freelancers." I had no idea I already had the connection to take me to the front door of my career!

STARTING FROM SCRATCH

My start in PR was full of discovering how little I knew. I freelanced for that PR business during lunch breaks, nights, and weekends on top of my full-time grant writer job. I didn't know how to operate as a freelance contractor, and I didn't know much about PR practice—which meant I didn't know how to write in Associated Press style or how not to embarrass myself with journalists during my first few pitch attempts. But I knew how to hustle, be resourceful, and adapt quickly. Within two months, the agency owners offered me the opportunity to work full-time in their boutique agency. I immediately accepted the role and have been in love with PR ever since.

What I know about PR now has been learned through humbling experiences. But bouncing back quickly from any missteps and trying not to make the same mistake twice has helped me to develop grit along the way. Supportive bosses, mentors, and Public Relations Society of America (PRSA) colleagues have been my workplace teachers throughout the years. I've filled in my professional gaps through industry volunteering, continued education, and by pursuing PR credentials such as the Accreditation in Public Relations (APR).

Designing my custom career path and figuring out which educational tools and relationships would complement it has been an exhausting, exhilarating, and worthwhile journey. All along the way, I could have felt like an imposter. I just never thought of myself as one. I thought I was lucky and still learning. To me, no one is an imposter unless they lie about their background and refuse to learn what they need to know.

Latinas, let's reject the popular label of "imposter syndrome." Unless you are a fraud, don't let yourself feel like a fraud. Do the work to learn what you need to, fix what is needed, or address what you need to so you can know inside that you're not an imposter. Embracing a growth mindset means you know there's always more to learn. We may never know everything, but we will benefit from pursuing lifelong learning and personal growth.

At the time of this writing, I am in my twenty-first year of working in PR. When I began writing this chapter, I was eagerly waiting to learn if I have earned the most elite credential in PR— being inducted as a member of the PRSA College of Fellows. I felt vulnerable about sharing that fact, because I did not know if I would be accepted as a Fellow in this attempt. Research shows that sharing our journey with others, particularly our mistakes, can be helpful to girls and women. At forty-four, I've been told I am "young" to be applying, given a pro becomes eligible to apply after twenty years in PR. Most professionals are closer to applying toward the sunset of their careers. But why not me, and why not now?

Sharing that I may not make a goal I've worked hard on could be helpful to someone. If I don't make it this time, I will try again. Perseverance, a superpower accessible to all, is probably my greatest asset.

Latinas must become comfortable with being among the first to do new things. Evolution means people shouldn't always do the same things in the same way. We must accept that we may have to try and then try again sometimes. Months later as I edit this chapter, I can share that I WAS accepted and officially inducted as a PRSA Fellow!

I hope my sharing this update inspires more Latinas to join me at that professional table. My making it means I can invite others to follow my journey. If you don't make it the first time, try, try again. But be prepared to be a first in many scenarios. Often, Latinas must be willing to take an important seat without an invitation.

DITCH DISCOMFORT AND CLAIM YOUR SEAT

When I worked in a corporation, I learned what it meant to be "tapped"—picked for a role or leadership opportunity. Being tapped made me think of some big, ominous being tapping some mere mortal on the shoulder. That suggested we wait to be viewed as worthy enough to get picked from among the crowd.

Well, we're no longer children waiting to be picked for gym class teams. I've learned that sometimes you have to pick yourself! Don't wait to get invited or tapped for a new role, job, or exciting opportunity. Stats imply that Latinas don't get picked as often as they should. We must raise our own hands, express our interests, and go after what we want ourselves.

I was not tapped for most of the exciting roles I am known for today. I either made the opportunity for myself or asked for it without an invitation. That's how I became a national columnist for PRSA! I pitched the editor using my PR skills to explain how I could offer a solution to an enduring representation gap in their publication. Often, I have found that people didn't realize I could, or wanted to be, of help.

No matter the cultural background, research shows that women need to work on embracing the necessary work of self-promotion to advance their professional and personal goals. Recently, three women-owned firms, Southpaw Insights, Mighty Forces, and Upstream Analysis, unveiled their findings from a national survey focused on the gender "self-promotion gap." The study examined the comfort and propensity of women and men to promote themselves and their accomplishments. Major findings showed that most women would rather minimize their successes than discuss them. The study surveyed 1,016 men and women eighteen and older, and identified trends across these groups, including:

- Only sixteen percent of women feel very comfortable talking about physical or athletic accomplishments.
- Forty percent of women would rather quit social media for a week than talk about themselves in public.
- Twenty-seven percent of women would prefer to visit the dentist than talk about themselves in public.

On top of most women's discomfort with self-promotion, Latinas grapple with a confluence of pressures. A study from Pew Research Center showed that more than half of Latinas say they often feel pressure to provide for their loved ones at home or succeed in their jobs. At the same time, they juggle cultural expectations around gender roles rooted in Latin America and in the United States. A majority of Latinas also said that US

Hispanic women face pressure to do housework, be beautiful, and start families. We have to be successful, family-focused, *and* beautiful?

VISIBILITY MOMENT

It's clear that feeling inferior can run rampant in our communities. Undervaluing our worth can lead us to act invisible at work and not reach for advancements. To help our families, succeed in our jobs, excel at PR, and feel more confident, we must push through discomfort to promote ourselves.

Here are some ways to get comfortable with discomfort and claim your seat:

- Accept that self-promotion is awkward (but effective).
- Think about who else you'll inspire.
- Focus on how to leverage spotlight opportunities.
- Manage your mindset to be adaptable and growth-oriented.
- Don't wait for an invite to the position, promotion, or party.
- Express your interest with enthusiasm.
- Accomplish big dreams in small steps.
- Pursue opportunities that seem out of reach.
- Determine your boundaries, set them, and protect them.
- Realize your point of view, voice, and life matters.
- Ask yourself, "Why not me? Why not now?"

Remember, the next generation may need to see you to one day be you. Leave a legacy worth following.

Melissa Vela-Williamson, MA, APR, Fellow PRSA, CDP

ABOUT THE MAIN AUTHOR/FOUNDER

Melissa Vela-Williamson is an accredited, internationally recognized public relations (PR) strategist, national industry columnist, podcast host, and author. For over two decades, she has provided strategic PR counsel, professional communication services, and shared leadership guidance with over one hundred brands—educating, equipping, and empowering diverse stakeholders ranging from children to chief executive officers (CEOs).

Melissa is a consultant, trainer, and account director at her boutique PR firm, MVW Communications. With unique experience in employee communications and diversity, equity and inclusion (DEI), Melissa leverages her PR expertise and acumen as a certified diversity professional to create social good. She is also certified by CompassionateUSA. Her first book, *Smart Talk: Public Relations Essentials All Pros Should Know,* was published in October 2022 and quickly became an Amazon bestseller.

Melissa's professional and lived experience influence her leadership perspective. Her self-driven nature, growth mindset, and tenacity have helped her develop a thriving personal and professional life. She's known for tackling tough topics, accomplishing hard things, and being a trustworthy, real-talk advisor for all types of people.

As a first-generation university graduate, first-generation PR practitioner, and first-generation business owner, she knows the nonlinear path to success many people pursue.

For more information on her or her firm's services, visit mvw360.com.

Melissa Vela-Williamson, MA, APR, Fellow PRSA, CDP

LinkedIn: Melissa Vela-Williamson

Websites: mvw360.com; latinasinpr.com

Acknowledgments

Saying thank you is the beginning of my expressing gratitude to all involved in this anthology's creation. First, thank you to all the new authors who joined me in bringing this book to life. You are the first public relations (PR) pros in Fig Factor Media's *Latinas in* anthology book series—much like you've been the first in your families, friends, or communities to take on so many inspirational challenges. I'm grateful for your trust in me and the time and effort you put into writing your stories. You have truly invested in yourself and helping others. Sharing your experiences will resonate, motivate, and empower readers. Audiences will see themselves in your chapters and can imagine that what you have achieved may be possible for them, too.

Thank you to Gini Dietrich, who advised me to connect with Priscilla Guasso. Gini saw my passion and commitment to inviting people of color, particularly those from the Latino community, to work in PR and to elevate their standing. She heard my struggles of driving myself through uncomfortable and new situations so I could share my call to action for more inclusion and advancement in the field.

Priscilla, the lead author of the *Latinas Rising Up in HR* anthology series, spoke with me about why and how she became the curator of these Latinas' stories. She also advised me when I wasn't sure I could make this book happen! Priscilla's books have led to the development of *Latinas Rising Up in HR* becoming a global movement with allies uniting across social platforms to represent Latina HR leaders worldwide.

Thank you to publisher Jackie Camacho-Ruiz for believing I would be a good steward of this collection, encouraging me through hard moments, and for allowing me to tailor this experience for our #PRtinas!

Much love and thanks to my husband, James, for supporting another of my big ideas and to my children, Emilia and Logan, who are my enduring motivation for doing scary things. Our children are showing us new ways to enjoy life, and I'm thankful that I can share my values and lessons with them so they can leapfrog past obstacles into promising, purposeful futures.

So many thanks go to my mother, Mary Frances Villa, for teaching me to work hard and to be resourceful.

Lastly, I thank God for this opportunity and the ability to express my thoughts via the written word.